(10)
WEEKS AT CHANUTE
A Discovery In Ruins

3703 BMTS
HONOR FLT 307
TSGT SEL HARDY
SSGT EAGAN
THE PICTURE SAYS IT ALL

LACKLAND AFB
12 JUNE 92

REN GARCIA

10 Weeks at Chanute
This book covers the experiences, recollections and inter-
pretations of the author while he attended basic training and
tech school at Chanute Air Force Base in 1992. The opinions
expressed within do not reflect those of the United States
military. The names of the Airmen who served with the author have been changed to protect their privacy.

Hydra
Publications

Published by Hydra Publications
ISBN: 978-1-942212-83-6
Printed in the United States of America
First Hydra edition: May 2017
Visit our website: http://www.hydrapublications.com

Table of Contents

Dedicated to all those places, long gone, that brings oneself into being.

10 Weeks at Chanute

The Author's BDU Shirt adorned with Staff Sergeant chevrons (near the end of his active tour) and maintenance squadron patch. These early 90's vintage BDUs were often known as 'Dog BDU's' because, as the story goes, the camouflage worked so well that a dog wouldn't be able to find you to piss on your leg.

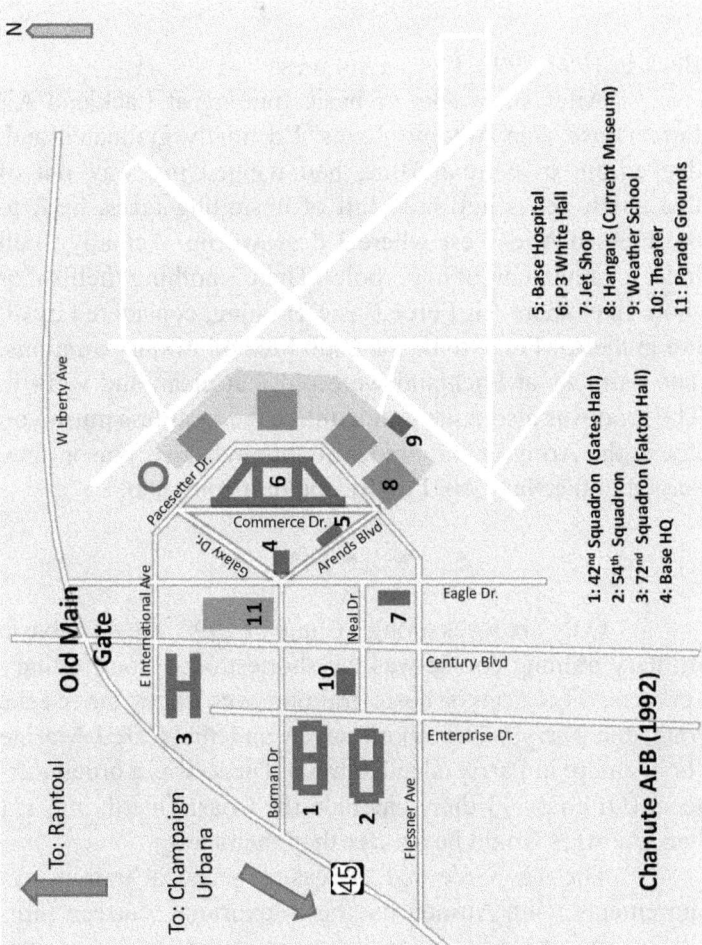

Chanute AFB (1992)

N

To: Rantoul

Old Main Gate

To: Champaign Urbana

45

W Liberty Ave

E International Ave

Pacesetter Dr.

Galaxy Dr.

Commerce Dr.

Arends Blvd

Neal Dr.

Eagle Dr.

Century Blvd

Enterprise Dr.

Borman Dr.

Flessner Ave

1: 42nd Squadron (Gates Hall)
2: 54th Squadron
3: 72nd Squadron (Faktor Hall)
4: Base HQ

5: Base Hospital
6: P3 White Hall
7: Jet Shop
8: Hangars (Current Museum)
9: Weather School
10: Theater
11: Parade Grounds

1

Those Heady Days

Back in 1991-1992, I was a hot mess.

After six weeks of basic training at Lackland Air Force Base, San Antonio Texas, I'd finally graduated and, decked-out in Airman Blue, had winged my way out of that south Texas hell hole full of unsmiling faces, back to the blessed Mid-West where I'd grown up. Actually, 'hell hole' is rather a bit of hyperbole. There's nothing 'hellish' or 'hole-like' about Air Force Basic Training, considered by all not in the Air Force to be the Club Med of military trainings. The barracks at Lackland were old, but clean and well-lit. The food was also quite good, unlike the toothless mush you got in the Army or the unidentifiable, reheated poison they served in the Navy, so, I really couldn't complain.

*　*　*　*　*

Only six weeks long in June of 1992, the AF's basic military training course was the shortest of all four military services. The Army's basic training was about ten weeks long, the Navy's was about seven and the feared Marine 'boot camp' in Parris Island and San Diego was a brutal thirteen. (Of course, I didn't include the Coast Guard, but, if I had, the AF's would be shorter than theirs too.)

The Air Force had the easiest physical training requirements, with Airmen having a luxurious fourteen minutes to run one mile. Every morning at the crack of dawn, scads of Airmen strolled around on the pad running circles for a mile, unless, of course, it was too hot and the black flag came out, in which case we didn't have to run. And, of course, a few couldn't do it, several unathletic Airmen falling out of the ranks and getting screamed at.

Every so often we had to do pushups. I remember the

lady TI coming over to me, leaning down, smelling of soap and powders.

She said in my ear: *"Get your pecker down, boy!"*

More easy stuff. You only had to run the obstacle course once, and it was mostly for show to go in the squadron year book. The Air Force also had the laxest gunnery standards of all the services, with trainees spending all of one afternoon on the dusty range with the M16 sending underpowered .22 bullets down range and eating 20 year old MRE's. I remember firing and firing, clouds of dust kicking up, wondering if I'd hit anything, and then almost getting a marksman medal for my trouble.

On the other hand, the Air Force required the highest ASVAB scores of all the services, was the most selective with its recruits, and played the most psychological havoc with its trainees.

"It's all a game," my TI, SSgt Hardy said at the end of it, a rare smile across her face as she inspected, for the final time, all the Airmen she had created. *"It's all just to see if you can take it. That's all we want to know ..."*

*   *   *   *   *

As the fussy, bumpy turboprop came down through the yellow, mid-summer haze, we all got excited, ready to wash Lackland's dust off our spit-shined shoes and continue on our Air Force adventure. Though I was mixed in with the other 'Blues', I was a bit different from the rest. I hadn't actually joined the Air Force, per say, instead I had joined the Ohio Air National Guard at the beginning of 1992. I was a Guardsman amid a bunch of Regulars.

Why did I do it?

I really didn't have much else to do.

*   *   *   *   *

1991-1992. Holy crap.

It was a momentous time in the country. We were on the restless edge unknowingly awaiting the seminal coming of the internet, the cell phone, the streamed data connection and the waiting canyons of social media. The Millennial Generation was pretty much entering their early teens by then. In comparison to today where our gadgets and the amount the Likes we collect make up much of who we are, we were still relatively (and blissfully) unplugged at the time. The economy was mildly recessed and jobs for new college graduates were a bit more scarce than usual. I was fresh out of the Ohio State University, armed with a diploma and an English degree, and not a good English degree that I could teach with—rather I had an English Lit degree. I wanted to write underground comic books with my friends, go to conventions, and play Dungeons & Dragons on my off days. I had a 20mg 8088 computer running C-DOS loaded full of my written, unpublished works (I still have it, actually, and it still works).

So, there I was, a 25 year old kid. I had my degree and my little hand-me-down car living in an apartment with my college buddies in Columbus, Ohio. I would hardly call myself a focused or independent person—none of us were. I'd been suckling at the parental teat the entire time, getting an allowance every week, calling home when I needed extra cash, the whole nine-yards. I hadn't really experienced much of anything. I'd been to school, but school is sort of a sheltered, nurturing kind of place, at least it was for me. I hadn't really been anywhere or done much of anything. I'd been deflowered, finally, at the age of 23 with a woman 12 years my senior who told me she loved me as we rolled around in the dark (the term 'Cougar' was unknown to me back then). Unfortunately, my folks, after 20+ years of constant support, decided enough was enough and cut me loose. A newly hatched pauper, I rolled around the vast campus of Ohio State, checking the rolodex in the rather tiny Job Placement Office off the Oval for plum assignments. The rolodex was a little light at the time. Most of the offerings for English grads regarded teaching English in Japan to Japanese who spoke no English, which sounds pretty appealing to me now, but back then I wanted nothing to do with it.

Having few viable prospects and a constant pair of

empty pockets, I pretty much had no idea what to do with myself. In 1991, I remember putting on my rumpled brown suit full of polyester snags and heading to a White Castle slider joint to apply for a manager's job. Down the tomb-like concrete stairs beneath the restaurant and through the dark door waiting at the bottom and my career as a professional burger-flipper would begin.

I never went down the stairs, I'm not sure what stopped me. Perhaps it was fear of having to be an adult at last. Perhaps it was pride, or maybe the first subtle notes of ambition bubbling to the surface, something I'd never been saddled with before.

A burger-flipper? Dude!

Who knows? I ended up working at a video store in Upper Arlington, renting VHS tapes to the locals which were all the rage at the time. There, I was treated to the nightly spectacle of Operation Desert Storm, President George H. W. Bush's grand master stroke in the Middle East. Desert Storm was a different sort of experience. There it was, plastered up on cable TV every night, live and green as an emerald in gaudy night vision. As a nation, we were collectively introduced to instant news, instant thrills, beginning our collective craving for all things quick and easy.

Just look at it on TV. We were kicking some major butt and looking good doing it. Desert Storm was a heady time and a perfect primer to the data storm that would soon transform all our lives. There it was: see what we as a country could do. Patriotism was reborn in greens and blacks, all at a new high since the end of the Cold War in 1989.

As the war ended, I got sick of being broke and working at the video store, so, I did what many people my age did—I folded my tent and went back home to live with my folks.

But, you really can't go back again, can you? With me sitting there, 25, gloriously unemployed, and doing little but playing video games all night, sleeping all day and eating food out of the pantry. 1991 stumbled unshowered into 1992. My folks had all sorts of ideas as to what I should do with my life. It was a daily argument that was brought to my childhood bedroom door with annoying frequency and I was, frankly, tired of hearing about it.

"Have you applied at store X?"

"You need a haircut."

"What is your status with Application Y?"

"Change your shirt…"

"You haven't seen the sun in months!"

Blah, blah, blah … I was finally starting to rebel and tune my parents out, not unlike many adolescents do, just belated by half a decade.

"Hey," my dad said in his tee-shirt one day at the table, "why don't you join the damn service?"

The service?

WTF?

My dad's golfing buddy was a Colonel at an Air National Guard base that I'd never heard of in nearby Spring

Grumman SA-16 Albatross

field, Ohio. "He's the commander of the base," my dad said (erroneously, I would find out later). I put down the video game controller and thought about it.

The service? My dad and most of my uncles had been in the service. My dad had been a radio man in a Grumman SA-16 (later HU-16) Albatross, an amphibious plane of the Korean War era used mostly for at-sea rescue operations.

I remembered seeing the slides of him as a young man standing there in his underwear with his buddies during a hurricane in Puerto Rico. He liked to dazzle me when I was a kid by banging out messages in Morse code with his finger on the kitchen table; I still remember SOS (... - - - ...). I used to thrill to the story he told me of how they had been sent out into the infamous Bermuda Triangle to search for a pair of drunken Swabbies who'd fallen overboard, and how my dad had been the one who spotted them from the air, peering out his tiny porthole, just a little pin-prick of guys in a tiny yellow raft floating on the living sea. My late uncle, Poncho, had been a warehouse guy and my other late uncle, Rene, had been a teacher for the Air Force. My youngest uncle, Cesar, was an SP/Air Policeman for the Air Force in Vietnam, where he had nearly been killed by a poisonous snake under a cot during a VC mortar attack (My uncle receives $666 dollars a month in compensation, plus COLA, courtesy the US government to this very day for that mortar-shell snake bite).

The Service?

I was still at a high from Desert Storm. All the things I'd seen on TV looked cool enough, I had nothing better to do, I had no money and my folks were driving me crazy on a daily basis. Even though none of my friends had joined the service, it seemed cool, seemed like an adventure. Perhaps joining the Air Guard and learning a trade would be good experience for me. Not like I had anything else going on, and anything was better than hanging out at my folks' house getting the stink ear every day.

It couldn't hurt.

I went out to the Springfield Beckley Municipal Airport and had a look around. It was a postage stamp of corrugated metal just past the utopian, tie-dyed village of Yellow Springs and safely isolated from the perpetual chaos of Springfield, the base was a huddled collection of ochre shacks and tin buildings surrounded by a rusty barbed wire fence and a sea of golden Ohio corn. There was a runway and a rickety tower squatting over the carcass of a tan Cold War-era hangar. There was an odd collection of obese, big-mouthed fighter planes painted sky gray lined up on the tarmac. I was whisked into a recruiter's office, where a hot, blonde-headed Senior Airman girl awaited me. Low on the formality and high on the flirtation, she started.

"Those are LTV A-7 Corsair II's out there," she said,

LTV A-7 Corsair II

"Those are naval tac-fighters."

Navy? I thought. Even back then I had a disdain for the US Navy. For me it conjured up images of Gilligan's Island, floppy hats and bad blue jeans. My disdain would grow as the years went by.

The dreamy blonde recruiter went on. "Don't worry about them, the A-7's I mean. They're going to the boneyard. The governor just approved us a whole squadron of F-16 Fighting Falcons. We'll be flying well into the 21st century with those."

The F-16. I was somewhat of an airplane buff, just one of my many passing interests, and I was familiar with the jet. General Dynamics' masterpiece. From scandal-ridden white elephant beset with developmental issues and cost-overruns to one of the best dogfighters ever flown in the jet age, the thought of working with a sexy, ballerina-like plane like the F-16 appealed to me.

The recruiter flirted with me for the rest of the afternoon and then set me up an appointment to take the **Armed**

Services Vocational Aptitude Battery or **(ASVAB)**—the standardized multiple choice test administered by the US Military to determine what jobs I could and could not safely do. The ASVAB was more than just an innocent test, it basically dictated one's fate in the military. What services you could join and what jobs you could do was forever determined by that seemingly innocuous little test. "You're going to want to score high, ok?" the blonde recruiter said.

I took the test several weeks later with a mixed bag of high school students, college guys and other assorted types dredged up from wherever. I don't recall the test being particularly difficult, though a few people sitting in the room with me were sweating profusely and looking around with their wide 'help-me' eyes as they took the test.

I then had to spend a long, humiliating afternoon at the **Columbus MEPS (Military Entrance Processing Station)** getting poked, prodded and ordered around by old men and angry, lips-pursed nurses to determine if all my limbs worked as normal, if my feet weren't flat and I had no STDs. I also had to show my rear-end to a crab-handed old man who wanted to know if I was gay or not. Needless to say, a day out at the MEPS was like a day stuffed in an anthill getting slowly eaten alive.

I was glad to find out everything on me works as normal.

A few weeks later my results were in: I had made the ASVAB my personal bitch. I could do anything I wanted. Now that it was proved that my brain and my body worked, I started getting lots of calls from other recruiters: from the Army, from the regular Air Force and … from the Navy too. Apparently a recruit with the MEPS behind him and a good ASVAB score was a prize worth seeking and I wasn't going to have the luxury of being left alone.

The calls I got from the Navy were sinister, rather arrogant and borderline creepy. "We're coming to get you," a voice on the telephone said. "We wanna' show you some things. You're going to love the Navy."

–CLICK—

Images of press gangs, Shanghai tunnels, metal

hooks, unconsciousness, and waking up a reluctant sailor aboard a westbound windjammer popped into my head and I couldn't get back with my little blonde recruiter out at Springfield fast enough.

The advantage of joining the Guard as opposed to going the regular Air Force route was you could hand pick exactly what you wanted to do ahead of time—the regulars didn't have that luxury. I would recall later at Basic Training during week 4, the fear and apprehension of my fellow class-mates as they waited to learn what AFC they'd been assigned to; their fate tacked up on the wall with striped tractor feed paper and dot-matrix print type.

The jostling. The bald heads bobbing around to see what was up.

"Where's mine? Where's mine?"

"A *cook?* I'm going to be a cook?"

"Where's Minot?? Oh God …"

"What the fuck …"

My dad's golfing buddy was the commanding officer of Logistics—the warehouse basically, and I couldn't see myself doing anything like that. It didn't interest me. Not in the least. The biggest shop on base was the engine shop, propped up with a number of stubby, coke-bottle shaped jets with a 'metal barrel' hanging on the ass-end (the venerable Allison/Rolls Royce TF41 turbofan 'Spey' motor, that I would come to know). I saw the gantries and swinging chains overhead like from a horror movie. The smell of the grease and oils rubbed into the old paint was thick in the air.

I was convinced. I wanted to be a Jetmech. "You've made a great choice," the recruiter said, "Since you have a college degree, you'll come in as an A1C (Airman 1st Class), or a two-striper instead of the usual slick-sleeves AB or, Airman Basic. You'll be shipping out for basic at Lackland AFB for six weeks in San Antonio, Texas. You're in luck as they're soon going to be adding two additional weeks onto basic training, but, right now, it's just six." (I'd heard that a lot in the up-

coming weeks, the old "we're adding two weeks onto basic training and when we wash you out you'll get to enjoy more time here!" It was a threat we got to listen to all the time. Eventually, years later, the Air Force actually followed up on the threat and added on two more weeks of basic. I have a nightmare every so often where I get hauled back to Basic in irons to get those two extra weeks under my belt).

"So, you'll go to Basic with the regulars, and then you'll be heading to Chanute Air Force Base to receive your Jetmech, or Aero-Propulsion Specialist training. It's a small little base in Illinois, about a hundred-some miles south of Chicago. You'll be there for ten weeks."

The recruiter didn't seem to think much of Chanute. "It's sort of … in the middle of nowhere. Yeah, it's No-wheresville, you know?" She rolled her eyes up and thought. "What's that place called, in China somewhere I think, the place in the middle of nowhere?"

I thought a moment. "Timbuktu, you mean? Old camel-train city. And it's in Africa, not China."

"Yeah, Timbuktu. It's like that. It's old and it's going to be closed by BRAC before too long."

"What's BRAC?" I asked.

"Base Relocation and Closure Committee. They were looking at us for awhile, before we got our new planes. You never want to get a visit from BRAC. You never want to be the base getting chopped. There's nothing sadder than a shut-down, chained up base. I know that because we almost became one of them. You'll be one of the last classes sent to Chanute. I wish you'd be going someplace else. There's Buckley, and Biloxi—I just love Biloxi, though it's sort of hot. You can always rent a car or take a bus to Chicago on the weekends—it's not so far. You can also take a bus into Champaign and hit Green Street at the University of Illinois if you want. You're a college guy, right? You'll fit right in."

The recruiter, the strapping blonde, seemed to be more interested in having fun and getting away from boring little Chanute AFB. She opined, in so many words, that to actually have to stay there over a long weekend when a paradise like Chicago was an easy drive away would be a total crap drudgery.

*   *   *   *   *

I didn't know it at the time, but sprawling, isolated Chanute had always been considered a 'crap' assignment, the worst the Army Signal Corps, the USAAF, and later the USAF had to offer a trainee. In the 1940's, getting assigned to Chanute with its decaying wooden buildings just a cast cigarette away from going up in a raging Hindenburg-like inferno in rural Illinois was akin to a dire punishment.

"Don't shoot 'em, Chanute 'em ... " they used to say. *"Got someone you don't want to deal with?? Send 'em and their dirty laundry to Chanute. That'll fix 'em but good."*

Timbuktu

Little did I know that those ten weeks I would spend at Chanute Air Force Base, the American Timbuktu on the plains in its last, dying days and destined to become a modern ruin, would haunt my soul to this very day.

2
A Whole Lot of Nothing

"Where's the F'ing base?"

The first time I saw Chanute, I was way sick: head cold, I'd gotten it from some Airman at Basic. The problem with living with fifty men in an open bay for six weeks is you share your diseases. The back-end of Basic Training deals with a lot of liberty and rolling around, as a result, you start getting sick. Real sick.

I got sick three times at Basic Training, each bout potent enough to make me feel half dead and pine away for my momma. What's worse, you couldn't mope around and feel sorry for yourself, and you certainly couldn't take a sick day. You had to keep going and you had to keep your ailments quiet.

Progress in Basic Training is measured in days, with each day having a specific set of tasks that had to be accomplished. If you missed a day, you had to make it up. A painfully easy way to 'wash back' in basic, is to get hurt. You get hurt, you go to the dispensary and then possibly the hospital and you start missing days that have to be made up later on, and nobody wants that. To have to wash back, or 'get recycled' as it was called a few days or a few weeks, is a misery. Although the TI's threaten to recycle you almost every day ...

"Gar-Fucking-cia, you're going to be packing your shit today, aren't you?" Sergeant Hardy would scream, egging me on all the time.

... there was a ton of paperwork and red tape involved with sending an Airman backwards, so the TI's generally tried to avoid the whole ordeal if possible. Don't get me wrong, if you pissed them off, or made enough work for them, they would get to it, do the paperwork, and recycle you. We lost about 35% of our original flight to recycling.

Of that number, about half of them recycled out due

to medical reasons. You want to get out of Basic Training as quickly as possible, and to go back or have to repeat the whole thing at a later time because you got hurt or sick is unacceptable. So, you hide your aches and pains and, quite literally 'soldier on'. I lost all feeling in my right foot as a result of my combat boots not fitting correctly. You march, march, march all day long at aptly-named 'boot camp', over here, over there, hurry up and wait, and my foot paid a terrible price. In the mornings, the shock of crashing out of my bunk for morning dress, my numb, pins and needles foot hitting the cold floor was pure agony ...

"FUCK!"

My mother, and my wife, often ask whenever I tell them of my pained foot at Basic why didn't I just return the ill-fitting boots?

Return the boots? This wasn't Macy's or JC Penney's—this was Basic Training. You didn't get to return anything. You took what they gave you and liked it, bad boots and all. You stood in line with your freshly shaved head, they'd eyeball you for a couple of seconds and give you what they thought would fit: your brown tee-shirts, your socks, tidy-whitey underwear, boots and your hot and cold BDUs (Battle-Dress Uniform). Getting those tightly folded brown tee-shirts on with your stubbly head for the first time was a real adventure, the cloth catching and holding fast to your dome like Velcro.

"Get those tee-shirts on, you fucking pukes! Get them on!"

So, you just stayed quiet and endured it. A flight brother of mine broke his leg and said nothing. Another guy got a raging case of The Clap from a San Antonio hooker and likewise said nothing. The TI's often shook us down, making us stand there in front of our racks in our undies checking for bruises, blisters, STDs and other assorted ailments and discolorations. Bumps and bruises meant fighting, blisters on the legs and groin meant sex and blisters on the feet meant bad boots.

Any of those things could send your ass backwards.

* * * * *

So, I was sick, head exploding, and I'd said nothing and taken nothing for it. I said goodbye to my flight brothers (I remember Sergeant Hardy standing there watching us leave. *"You packing your shit today, Garcia?"* she asked with a small bit of hard-won affection. *"Ma'am, yes, ma'am,"* I replied)

…and boarded the turboprop plane with a handful of people. With bleary caul-like eyes, I watched the uninteresting yellow landscape of the Great Plains pass below, a collage of huddled golden squares stretching out on a flat landscape as the plane made its way north.

I remember the dry air and pressure in the airplane really made my head pound. Soon the plane came down and I saw a small airfield emerge from the gloom—the first thing I saw was the large 'X' the runways made on the ground. I felt a weird sort of dread as the plane came in to land. As the recruiter back at Springfield had told me, I saw little below but the X-shaped airstrip and a few, squared-off side roads and buildings, everything relentlessly yellow in hue. I had no idea what to expect, or what to do. A funny thing—you get used to people shouting orders at you. Your brain shuts down and you become accustomed to having your entire waking day regimented. It's easy to stop thinking for yourself and simply react to things around you. Suddenly being liberated to some extent, feels wrong, seems weird, and isn't entirely welcome.

Somebody give me an order…

The plane landed, the door opened admitting the usual Mid-Western glare that I knew so well. Stepping off the plane into the blinding sunshine, I was shocked. I saw, literally, nothing. There was the tight grain concrete of the runway, still kept pristine and debris-free even though the Air Force hadn't used it as a functional air strip in a long time. Way off in the shimmering distance was a silvery hangar, like an alien pyramid rising up out of the desert. Besides the hanger, the plane we'd just landed in and us milling around in our blues, there was nothing. Coming from Ohio, I thought I knew what flat ground was, however, the Illinois landscape was flat enough to play a game of pool on. It was like it had been steamrolled by God's fist at the beginning of time, then flipped off in passing as he strode away to more interesting places.

View from Chanute's rather lonely tarmac, giving one the distinct feeling of being abandoned. (RDG)

Where's the base, I wondered. Air Force bases are always littered with larger than life mementos: statues of dead men, plaques, mounted obsolete aircraft pooped on by generations of birds, donated trees, etc. I was familiar with Wright-Patterson AFB as both my parents worked there, and Wright-Patt was rotten with ceremonial 'stuff' left and right. I didn't see any of that at Chanute; a sea of flatlands, a silvery hanger, a runway, a plane, us, and that was all. I imagined this was sort of how standing on Mars might look.

We stood there wondering what was going on as our baggage came off the plane. Were we at the right base?

After a while a bus drove up, a guy got out, yelled at us and ordered us in. I have no idea who that fellow was. He could have been anybody, a bum, a general, the president, a serial killer—no clue. I followed his commands without question and got on the bus.

He drove off the lonely runway past the hangar and eventually we saw signs of life, there were new and old metal buildings and streets and landscaping. Ah! There was an old B-58 Hustler parked on a green, manicured concourse—typical Air Force. There were red-brick buildings and flag poles sporting Old Glory. Though small, Chanute was a typical, modern Air Force base after all.

We were driven down several streets to a large red brick dormitory built in a functional, squarish, somewhat ugly style. We got out with our baggage, lined up and were marched through a courtyard. Airmen were lounging about in their BDU's and half BDU's, some chewing, others smoking like dragons. They watched us come in.

I saw one and acknowledged him with a nod.

"Ping!" was his reply.

Ping? What's Ping I wondered?

"Ping?" another airman said.

"Ping," another one.

Ping, Ping, Ping, PING! PING!

It was like the buzzing of a swarm of green insects: Ping, Ping Ping! PIIIIIINNNNNNNNNGGGGGGGGGGGGG!!! We were being peppered with it. Some of the more adventurous dudes waving pool sticks around hit us hard with a rousing "Waaaa-Pinggg!!"

What was this? Some sort of initiation? Some sort of hazing?? What the heck was all this "Ping! Ping!" crap? All I knew was I didn't like it. I felt picked-on and exposed. I was in no mood for it. (I never would learn the history and true meaning of the word 'Ping' and why it was uttered in such a hostile fashion to newbies freshly arrived at the base. If you were new to the base, you were a Pinger, that's all there was to it, and, to those ahead of you in weeks at Chanute, you never really stopped being a Pinger.)

We were led into the dormitory and taken to the CQ. "I got a new batch of Pingers here," he said, "and they're a real treat." The CQ signed for us and we were led into a small room with chairs. A bald eagle mural was painted on the far wall with the words SPECIAL ACTIVITIES highlighted beneath it.

We sat and waited. After a few minutes we heard the familiar 'tap … tap … tap' of approaching footsteps. The

TI's at basic wore taps on their boots so that you could hear them coming, and that was a sound I wasn't expecting. Good God, I'd thought we were done with that.

A young MTM with a Cary Grant 'do came in. An MTM (Military Training Manager) was sort of a laid-back TI who oversaw whole squadrons of trainees. You usually didn't see them too often, unless you got into trouble somewhere, usually by missing classes, chalking up bad grades, being caught where you weren't supposed to be, etc. If any of those things happened, then you'd see the MTMs a lot.

He looked us over and gave a perfunctory welcome to Chanute in an uninterested voice.

"Any of you Pingers play a musical instrument?" he asked in a slow twang.

I'd been told by my fellows at the Guard Base in Springfield that an easy way to get out of the rock-pounding drudgery at Basic was to join the Band Flight. They told me that, at the beginning, your TI (or MTI: Military Training Instructor—the Demons of Lackland) will ask if anybody plays a musical instrument. Just say 'yes' and then they'll transfer you out of where you are and into the Band Flight, which generally was thought to have a pretty easy time of it compared to everybody else. As a bewildered Rainbow at Basic, I kept waiting for the crazy little black woman with the hat screaming at us to say: "Any you sumbitches play a goddamn instrument other than your dicks?"

I play the trumpet. I was in marching band in high school. I kept thinking: *I'm getting out of here and going someplace soft.*

Bye bye, baby.

Trouble was the TI never asked and I was stuck there. I lay there the first night in my rack staring at the ceiling wondering when I was getting out, and it never happened. In fact, our TI was pretty brutal about things like that. She never asked about the instrument thing, she wouldn't let us have sweets or desserts in the chow hall or at the rifle range and she even fired all the guys who were there for three week ROTC honors flight and made them do the whole tour.

So, there I was six weeks later sitting in a little room

at Chanute being asked the question I didn't get asked at Basic by a shifty guy with nice hair. "Do you play an instrument?"

The MTM talked about the Special Acts being an elite unit and morale was high because everybody in it wanted to be there. I thought about it, but ultimately said nothing. I was sick (literally) and tired and the last thing I wanted to do was hoist a trumpet up to my aching face. I sat there and remained mum. The MTM gazed at us, at me in particular. I wondered for a moment if he could read my mind and intuitively knew I played an instrument. I wondered if I had a 'band nerd' sort of look. I kept the thought buried and silently repeated the mantra my Springfield Guardsmen had taught me before shipping out to avoid being noticed by authority types:

No eye contact. No noise. No sudden movements.

I figured I got through Basic just fine not being in the Band Flight, I'd be fine here as well. Airman Westridge, a little guy from Virginia who went through Basic with me, spoke up. "Yeah, yeah I play the piano." I thought for a second he was going to rat me out as a trumpet-player, as I had told him I played at Basic. Westridge didn't say anything, and he was taken away.

I later found out the Special Acts was a rather maniacal outfit, high on spit and polish and rather secretive as to their ways—sort of like the instrument-playing, rifle twirling Gestapo of Chanute. If you had words with any of them, they'd gang up on you later. Westridge got beaten up pretty good, though he eventually grew to like it and wore his starched BDU's with pride.

The sinister encounter with the Special Acts guy over, we were taken to a different part of the dormitory into a dark room that seemed to have been a stage at some point for it had adjustable lighting on gantries suspended overhead.

My nose was plugged, my sinuses killing me. I wanted to be shown to my room or bay or whatever and that was all. So far, I couldn't stand this place and harbored dark thoughts of wanting to return to Lackland. The whole scene had a real `70's vibe: the décor, the materials, the stale smells, it was like being stuck in an old man's closet, and I wanted out.

A lady MTM came out and gave us the skinny that I only partially listened to. We were among the last classes to come to Chanute, she said. The place was done—chopped. The various schools were getting ready to shutdown and ship out.

She mentioned something about the Dalai Lama buying the place, or maybe a religious cult from Texas, but I wasn't listening at that point. Whatever. Let whoever have it. Take it all.

Hearing all this talk of shipping out and shutting down, I had a creepy sort of feeling simmering in my gut—like when you've missed your plane or your bus and you're stranded someplace far from home, left behind with no clear idea how you were getting out of it. I felt shipwrecked in the middle of Illinois, with rescue being a distant 10 weeks away. 10 weeks might as well be 10 years. As we were shuttled out of the dark room to have our first meal at Chanute, by that point I was in full-on homesick mode. I wanted desperately to go back to the open bays and familiar laughs of my flight at Lackland, or possibly go home. I was convinced I wouldn't like Chanute much and my stay there would be 10 weeks of pure, unmitigated hell.

Funny how things start sometimes.

3
A Generalized History of Chanute

Learn something, ok ...

Chanute Air Force Base is located on the southern edge of Rantoul, Illinois in Champaign County. It's a relentlessly flat and rural place. Chicago, a hundred thirty miles to the north, is an urban aberration; Illinois is a quiet rural state, naturally as flat as a soccer pitch, and the Rantoul area is every bit of that and more.

The main base in its final configuration was comprised of a little more than 2000 acres butted up against a railroad to the west and a squarish Heritage Lake to the south, though, in its humble beginnings as a temporary airfield, it was only about 600 acres. Throughout its life, Chanute was a place of training and research for Army officers, pilots, Air Force officers, Airmen, civilian employees, and for other Department of Defense agency personnel. Many people came and went over the decades, all of them came for training, to learn.

"Learn something, ok?" my boss, a Senior-Master Sergeant at the guard base said to me as I went off to Basic.

Learn something. That's what Chanute was there for, to teach. Training activities focused on operation and maintenance of military aircraft and ground support equipment, AGE equipment, weather forecasting and fire training.

It was established on May 21, 1917 as the Rantoul Aviation Field. It was initially used by the Army Signal Corps as a place to train pilots to fly those new, under-powered wood and cloth deathtraps known as airplanes. Congress had appropriated a fair amount in assets to 'build up the Air Service'. Aviation at that time in the old military was not looked upon with much regard, and few heads in the brass could divine much use for the new, rickety flying contraptions beyond light scouting and reconnaissance.

Even as World War I tore through Europe and the

airplane began to assert itself as the harbinger of destruction over the trenches, the hidebound brass in the US did little to promote its development. Thus, the little field in the middle of nowhere south of Chicago meant give a half-hearted nod to the air service and to train a few scouts to fly them for after-thought missions that they probably wouldn't survive anyway.

In April, 1917, though American airpower was non-existent, the French, in contrast, had a 1500 aircraft armada to fight the Germans with a handful of great planes: the Moraine-Saulnier, the Spad, the Nieuport. The frightful pusher-style monstrosities stumbling into the skies at the beginning of the war were replaced by truly competent aircraft as the French and British sought to keep up with and outdo the hated Germans in a bloody test of gamesmanship.

There was little aviation innovation going on in the US. The Wright Brothers had familiarized the world to heavier-than-air flight, but nothing much happened after that. In 1916 the first largely American fighting unit was formed in Luxeuil-les-Bains, France to take on the Germans called the 'Lafayette Escadrille', and these American pioneers flew into battle in French planes: the Nieuport 11. The American creed of flying and fighting its own aircraft would not take hold for another few decades.

In 1917, flush with cash, the War Department opened several schools across the country to train scouting pilots. It established schools at several colleges and laid ground at over twenty air fields, the Rantoul Aviation Field being just one of them. Its remote location was selected for several reasons. One, the ground there was level and generally tree-free and would be ideal for taxiing. Two, the field could make use of the nearby village of Rantoul for power and water needs, and, three, the site was a short country drive to the University of Illinois, which also sported a ground/flight school. The field's proximity to the Illinois Central Railroad was another plus.

The field was completed in July, 1917 at an approximate cost of one million dollars. The paint wasn't even dry and the first plane hadn't even landed before it was decided to effect a name change to the field: Chanute Field.

Octave Chanute was a true pioneer of aviation and an Illinois eminence. Born in France in 1832, Chanute, like many, immigrated to the United States as a young man to make his fortune. He became known as an innovative railroad engineer. He designed the massive Chicago and Kansas City stockyards and also a number of key bridges, helping to establish Kansas City as a railroad hub. He developed a system of pressure-treating wooden ties to increase their durability and service life and the 'date nail' to help track their age.

In 1875, Chanute became interested in aviation during a visit to Europe, and, having retired from railroad engineering, decided to devote his free time to that pursuit. In 1894, he published an influential book called: *Progress in Flying Machines,* which, at the time, was the most complete survey of the state of heavier-than-air research available.

He began developing a series of hang gliders that featured a number of key innovations, namely the use of a strut-braced wing, and a stacked, dual wing configuration that would become widely known in later years as the 'biplane'. Chanute's creations, to our modern eyes, looked like they would fly, unlike many of the earth-bound contraptions being developed at the time. Also, unlike other aviation pioneers, heady to make the papers, Chanute kept his old, retired boots on the ground, leaving the testing of his gliders to other, younger people.

Chanute was a close advisor to the Wright Brothers, and his 1896 dual-winged hang glider was a direct progenitor of the Wright's iconic Kitty Hawk Flyer, they share a clear resemblance.

As Chanute was from the area, it followed that his name be honored by re-naming the new air field Chanute Field.

When World War I ended in November, 1918, a frequent and oft-revisited topic came up regarding the future of the field: closure. The Great War was over and certainly nothing like it would ever be seen again. What was the further use of a military air field? Why sink another dime into it? But, Congress intervened and, in 1920, approved funding to purchase Chanute Field. In 1922, nine steel hangars were constructed on the southern frontier of the original field to permanently house planes. In 1923 Hangar 10 was completed and represented the last major construction effort at the field for the next fifteen years. Though small and remote,

Chanute was the only field base in the tiny Army Air Arm to offer technical training from 1922 until 1938.

As the decades passed, Chanute's mostly wooden construction and dilapidated condition saw the outbreak of many fires leaving the field a pile of ashes several times. After each inferno, the topic of abandoning the field was discussed, and, as before, the Army Air Corps again decided to rebuild. In 1938 many new buildings were added, including two massive hangers, a giant 300,000 gallon water tower, a hospital, a barracks, several warehouses, a fire station, and officer's quarters. This great period of growth was funded by President Roosevelt's Works Progress Administration (WPA). In addition, several theatres, more barracks, family housing facilities, a gym and a modern concrete runway were added. All this growth was completed in 1941, just months before the Japanese attack at Pearl Harbor.

In the aftermath of the attack, many citizens flocked to Chanute to enlist. The brand new 15,000-man quarters built during the heady period of growth known as 'Buckingham Palace' could not house them all and many had to be setup in tents near the lake. Chanute's student population grew to a peak of 25,000 in 1943.

The field acquired its current name, Chanute AFB, in 1948.

After the war, decay set in and Chanute once again became a dilapidated, unpleasant place huddled by the railroad in Rantoul. It was so decrepit that Rantoul considered it an embarrassment. Being sent to Chanute was considered either a demotion or an outright punishment. *"Don't shoot 'em, Chanute `em"* became the general derogatory catch phrase, where assignment to the dreary base was considered only slightly less favorable to execution.

But, Chanute refused to die and world events played into its favor. The conflict in North Korea brought about another period of growth for Chanute, as the newly formed United States Air Force needed training sites for its recruits.

Having more lives than the proverbial cat, Chanute became the prime training center for the LGM-30 Minuteman intercontinental ballistic missile program—one of the most important in the US military's history. The Minuteman was the centerpiece in NATO's missile deterrent program against the Soviet Union (I always wondered what a giant white missile was doing mounted at the Borman Gate of the base near my dorm). Chanute was a beehive of activity, training not only the US Airmen, but those from Asia and the Middle East as well.

During Vietnam, Chanute provided training for thousands of Airmen serving overseas. The base saw new life, investing heavily in new student dormitories, quality-of-life programs and other support programs. In 1971, it became the prime training center for the ALCM program (Air-Launched Cruise Missile), including the GLCM (Ground-Launched Cruise Missile) and the MX.

Missile situated at the old Borman Gate serves as a reminder of Chanute's role in the Air Force's ICBM program. (RDG)

There seemed to be no end to the training uses Chanute could fulfill, however, in 1971, the first of many setbacks occurred that would eventually spell the end of the facility. The runway, due to a cessation of aircraft support, was shut down. Chanute became an air field with a non-working runway. It didn't seem like a big deal at the time as the base was a training facility, but more 'shutdowns' would follow in the years ahead.

With the introduction of the Pratt & Whitney F-100 turbofan used in the F-15 and F-16 aircraft, Chanute was flooded with new training courses to remain on top of the rapidly changing equipment students would be servicing in the field. (I myself trained on the PW F100, however, in the field our planes were fitted with the GE F-110, a totally different animal, therefore my training was thrown out the window).

From 1983 to 1992, if you were a Jetmech turning wrenches on a jet engine in the USAF, you went, mostly, to Chanute. The J-57, the prehistoric power plant of the prolific and long-lived B-52 was taught there, as well. Not only that, Chanute hosted a turboprop school, which my good friend from Basic, Matt Fujimoto, attended. It hosted AGE and warehousing schools, the USAF firemen learned to put out runway fires there, C130 pilots practiced short landing and air drops on the now disused airstrip.

In 1985, Chanute consolidated the Aircraft Environmental/Pneudralics and Electrical Systems division. It truly seemed there was nothing this little base in Illinois couldn't do.

But then, after educating literally thousands of students, winter fell on Chanute and its luck ran out.

On December 29th, 1988, the DOD (Department of Defense) recommended Chanute's closure as an active base, mostly as a cost-saving measure. Chanute had flirted with base closure many times, first on account of peace-time, and then because of fire, then because of dilapidation, and then because of the end of the Cold War. Chanute had no flying mission, its location was remote and odd for an airbase, and the time had come to shut it down. The base was old, having 75 years of proud tradition and was the oldest USAF training center and the third oldest base overall.

Done deal. The USAF had given up on Chanute. When the Iron Curtain came down, so too did the base and it was left to die. It closed on September 30th, 1993, a little over one year after I attended classes there. All the various schools drifted away to other bases. The Aero/Mech school I attended would be transferred to Sheppard AFB in Texas.

4
Dehydration and Constipation

I settled into my dorm room in the 'Thundering' 42nd squadron where most of the prolific Jetmech students were housed. It was a plain, 50's era red-brick building on the corner of Borman and Enterprise drives, three floors high, built in a figure 8 with two grassy courtyards in the center divided by a large window-strewn dayroom where everybody hung out. 'Gates Hall' was hung in shiny letters over the main lobby doors. A missile painted white near the Borman Gate, one of three main gates at the base, stood watch over the dorm like Octave Chanute's raised bony finger up from the grave.

Gates Hall, the 42nd Squadron dormitory located on the corner of Enterprise and Borman Drives looking a little witchy in 2012. Through the breezeway was a courtyard leading to the dayroom in the center. (RDG)

✳   ✳   ✳   ✳   ✳

A quick note on Air Force organization.
Being a huge entity comprised of many people doing

many different things, the Air Force is divided into a number of sub-units, each getting progressively smaller until you're down to a single Airman. A single person in the Air Force, no matter who that person is, is an Airman. Two or more Airmen are known as a Section, (or Element). If you have four Elements, you have a Flight. Put two or more Flights together, you have a Squadron. If you have two or more Squadrons, you have a Group, put two or more Groups together, you have a Wing. There's usually only one Wing per base, and the Wing Commander is usually the Base Commander. After that, you get into the huge Numbered Air Force (8th Air Force, 10th Air Force, etc), which are mostly obsolete, and then the various commands.

Whew! That's a lot of stuff. As a trainee, I really wasn't aware of most of that. At Basic, I knew my Flight, the 307th, but didn't really know what Squadron I was in, and at Chanute, it was the opposite, I knew my Squadron, the 42nd, but had no clue what Flight I was in (my Flight was whatever group of guys I lined up with to march out to class). On my graduation certificate, it says my Jet Mech course was conducted by the 3330th Training Wing. Fine. Whatever. Meant absolutely nothing to me at the time.

The Squadrons were what I knew. My Squadron, the 42nd, Matt Fujimoto's, the 72nd, and then there was the 54th, the enemy. Why they were the enemy, I'm not really sure. They just were. I'm also embarrassed to say, I'm not totally certain I'm remembering the 54th correctly—I was only there for three months over twenty years ago. I'm *pretty sure* it was the 54th. It was in the 50's, I'm positive of that. In all the research I did to refresh my memory, I could find nothing one way or the other, so, until I learn otherwise, it's the 54th. If anybody out there knows better, just let me know and I'll revise. Promise.

∗   ∗   ∗   ∗   ∗

The 42nd wasn't much to look at, but the paint on the walls was flawless, the floors buffed to a high shine—the Air Force was always big on clean walls and buffed floors. My room was on the first floor, just a hard left turn down the way from the CQ's desk in the squadron lobby. Inside my room were two desks, two old wood-frame beds (with incredibly squeaky springs, which I was told were there to sound the alarm in case you were attempting to have unauthorized sex on them), a radiator and a closet. The beds had those God-awful green military blankets from the 1930's, thin, scratchy—like wool from a brillo pad's ass, stamped with 'US' that you had to hide from view—you'd get a demerit if your bed was inspected and the US stamp was showing. The common latrine was just a few paces further down the hall.

You were supposed to keep your room up to military standards—no clutter, no clothes lying around, your bed made nice and tight every day, BDUs pressed, boots shined. You never knew when you were going to be inspected by the MTMs. I honestly don't recall anybody ever inspecting my room the entire time I was there. The base was readying to close, the MTMs were all trying to figure out where the hell they were going to land, their presence around the squadron became less and less as the weeks went by to almost not at all at the end. They might have inspected my room while I was away at class, but nobody ever said anything and I never got in trouble once. In fact, the worst trouble I got while at Basic/Tech School was in regards to an electric razor plugged into an outlet at Basic. The TI's raised holy hell over it and, as the foolish Dorm Guard who allowed the offending razor to remain, I had to write sentences, 100 times:

"I swear I will not allow my incompetence as an Airman to endanger the lives of my fellow trainees ever again."

Tech school was a way different experience from Basic. Unlike Basic, there was no morning cow-call to get you up at Chanute. Every morning, you got up on your own, dressed in your BDUs and lined up in the yard to march to your classes, usually down Borman Drive which led into the heart of the base. If you were smart, you'd go down to the BX and buy yourself an alarm clock and keep your hair cut way short—not having hair to deal with in the morning was a big time-saver.

I still remember it was a hell of a sight every morning, seeing all the Airmen in their fresh green BDU's and black combat boots rolling around on the grass, smoking, grab-assing, waiting to go to class. Everybody carried a standard-issue brief case containing your course work, your writing materials, your demerits in case you got in trouble, and your raincoat in case it rained. I remember every morning smelled like it had just rained, a little Illinois mist rolling across the ground, giving it all a slightly damp, surreal appearance. It was just like my days at Ohio State, everything was on your own initiative, with the exception that there was hell to pay if you missed class or if you earned poor grades. Your mission at Chanute was to go to school, and missing class or getting sub-standard grades would bring the MTMs to your door, extra duty on the weekends, and possibly a visit to CC (Correctional Captivity, otherwise known as jail).

After living with fifty men in an open bay for six weeks, living with just one other guy was amazing. I quickly regained my former independence, and, something else too, a thin glimmer of something I didn't have before: responsibility. I learned where I could go and not go without getting into trouble. I learned about the dangers of Chanute, bandied about every afternoon by seasoned Airmen in the 42nd dayroom. You couldn't walk in the interior of the base by yourself, especially near the Bermuda Triangle, the confluence of Galaxy Drive, Arends Boulevard and Commerce Drive where the Base HQ, the Hospital and the giant-sized Building P3, otherwise known as White Hall, were located. Sour-faced permanent party officers buzzed around the Bermuda Triangle like hornets ready to sting to death any foolish trainee who blundered in. It was a place you had no business going. I had stripes on my sleeves, and with my sleeves bloused up, it was difficult to tell if I was an A1C, a Senior Airman or a Staff Sergeant, so I was a little more difficult to pick out as a trainee, but still, why tempt fate?

In any case, when out and about, walking alone at Chanute was forbidden. As a Chanute trainee, you had to march with your Flight, or in a paired Element, at all times, or you had to have a Straggler's Pass which was a coveted thing to have. Airmen walking alone often got stopped by the MTMs or by officers and were compelled to show them their papers. Even if alone and you had a pass, you couldn't just walk down the sidewalk, you had to march: straight up, good posture, perform facing movements, no 'rubber-necking', the whole smack required of soldiers that civilians didn't have to worry about.

Was it a pain? Yes, but damn, what a thing to see every morning, the mist of a fresh new day laced with a hint of tobacco, the blocks of resplendent green Airmen lined up in parade order marching down Borman and Enterprise drives to their classes, the flight and squadron leaders with their green, yellow or red command ropes pinned to their shoulders barking marching orders, sometimes singing to set the cadence.

> *"Squadron!"*
> *"Flight!"*
> *"At my command!! Who are you?"*
> *"A Jetmech, sir!"*
> *"What do we do?"*
> *"Fly, Fight and Win!"*
> *"Chanute!"*

The immaculate red buildings, the trim grassy areas right out of some rural county in Ireland, the hypnotic CHUCK, CHUCK, CHUCK of the collective boot heels of young men and women hitting the ground in unison down the orderly, well-maintained streets, the outside world fenced off, kept at bay. Chanute was a little bit of precision operating without fail every morning in an imperfect world.

I remember seeing various people standing on the sidewalks watching us assemble and march out to class every morning. I remember wondering why they were so fascinated. What was the rumpus about?

Why? Because a morning at Chanute with its intricate ins and outs, the shouted orders, its structured chaos and Airmen marching down the street with ground-shaking synchronization, was a damn thing of beauty.

∗   ∗   ∗   ∗   ∗

Twenty years later, I would stand in those same streets all by myself, looking at those same buildings sunk deep in silence, regaled by the ghosts of what once was, and I recall having tears in my eyes for what was lost and would never be again.

∗   ∗   ∗   ∗   ∗

The area around the dorms was a safe spot where you could walk by yourself—venture too far from the dorms, enter the Bermuda Triangle, and you were in jeopardy of getting nicked. I located a small BX nearby where I could buy snacks and take them back to my room. I remember basking in the solitude of my room with the A/C cranked up, wrapped up in those crappy green blankets luxuriously eating candy and reading about Prince Charles and his new love, Camilla Parker-Bowles from a magazine I'd bought. If it was the weekend, I could sleep in if I wanted. I also bought a steam iron at the BX (which I still have after all these years) so I could cheat when shining my combat boots by heating my shoe polish to a liquid and dabbing it on with a wet cotton ball—much easier that way and forbidden back at Lackland where you had to polish your boots with nothing but elbow grease. (We didn't have Desert Boots back then. Our boots were leather and black and we had to spend a lot of time shining them). I didn't go too far, and I didn't go off base much at the beginning because I'd have to get into my Blues. Per the **UCMJ** (Uniform Code of Military Justice) you weren't allowed to wear your BDU's off base unless you were working. If you went out, you had to be either in your civilian clothes or in your dress Blues. I still remember getting the drill from our instructors:

"If I catch any of you people out in the city shopping in your BDU's I'm pulling your card (Military ID). *If you're coming to or from work, you can stop at a convenience store and you can get milk, or you can get lunch meat, or you can get milk AND lunch meat, but if you get anything else, you're*

... shopping."

I also discovered all the convenient places to hide should retreat sound. When retreat sounded, which was at the beginning, middle, and end of every work day, Airmen walking down the sidewalk would literally dive for cover to get out of having to stand and salute—it sort of looked like an air raid with bodies flying everywhere. If you couldn't find cover or a suitable place to hide, and you were caught outside, you could expect to spend a long five minutes or so at attention saluting the flag as the National Anthem was played over the bull horn.

Another luxury seldom appreciated by civilians, I could go to the latrine whenever I wanted and not have to ask permission. Unchallenged, and with facilities available, I was constipated no longer.

✳   ✳   ✳   ✳   ✳

A note on pooping.

Basic Training plays havoc on your system. I remember sitting there in the little cubbyhole in the San Antonio airport with Matt Fujimoto, an affable fellow from Honolulu, Hawaii waiting for them to come and pick us up. I'd used the one-way plane ticket they'd given me, and there I was, sitting in the cubbyhole with Matt waiting to get taken away. He had brought a vast bag full of treats and he was eager to share. Sitting there eating junk food, I marveled how easy it would be to simply get up and walk out of the cubby hole, to blend in with everybody else at the airport that day, and nobody would be the wiser. I could have skipped out on Basic Training. It was tempting, but, something kept me in there, nailed to my seat, to willingly subject myself to the horrors to come.

Matt's bag of junk food took its toll. After awhile, I had to use the restroom, bad. Prairie dog bad. I figured I'd wait until I got to the base—if I left the cubby, I might not come back.

So, I held it.

When they finally came and got us, they marched

us out with our baggage and loaded us up on an old-style school bus painted Air Force blue. We were all Rainbows in our multi-colored civilian clothes and this was the beginning of our Air Force experience. It was over a hundred degrees on the bus and all the windows were up, so it was stifling. In a normal situation, your first inclination would be to lower a window and get some air, however this was not a normal situation, was it? We were heading to Boot Camp. We all looked at each other and silently wondered if the closed windows were a test of some sort and bad things awaited he or she dumb enough to try and open one.

Everything is a big deal over there, the fellow Guardsmen in Springfield had told me, so, I figured opening a window might be considered a big deal. Other people must have thought the same thing, we just sat there and sweated, all except for Matt, he fussed and struggled with his window, slapping at it, puzzling over it, sweat pouring off his face. He never did get it down as the bus relentlessly sped us toward Basic Training.

When we got to the base, this young TI in a Smokey the Bear hat lined us up, suitcases and all, on a pad full of painted footprints.

He spoke. His voice was like a steel-toothed bear trap dragged across a gravel road. "When I say your name, reply 'Sir here, sir!' Got it?" he rasped. He started reading names off a clip board.

"Adams!" he said.

"Sir, here, sir!!"

"Allen!"

"Sir, here, sir!!"

"Anderson!"

No response.

I could see his angry eyes peek up over the top of his clipboard. "Anderson!" he said again.

There was a pained sort of gurgle, and then someone behind me said "Here, sir, here!" instead of the required "Sir, here, Sir!"

As we were soon to find out, it was the little things like that that set these TI's off.

Everything's a big deal, they had said back in Springfield, and that was proved the first ten minutes of Basic.

Fire came from the TI's eye sockets and he pushed his way past me into the ranks of terrified Rainbows to get at Anderson.

"Jesus H. Goddamn Christ!" he roared. "If I didn't get stuck with another boatload of pukes, didn't I? I just got off the phone with your mama, and she told me you were dumb, but Jesus! You're not here five minutes and you're already fucking up! Now, say it right, you worthless piece of crap! We'll try it again! ANDERSON!!"

"Here, sir, here!" the terrified Anderson said again.

"GODDAMMIT!" the TI roared, throwing his clipboard down. And he took Anderson by the shoulder and led him away and I never saw him again. I'm assuming Anderson is still alive out there somewhere today, though I have no proof of that.

After that I was in quite a state. I forgot all about my belly full of junk food, the bathroom and my need to visit it. It was as if my body tucked into itself and re-absorbed what I needed to excrete just to keep me from having to use the potty and face the wrath of a TI. That night I lay there in my rack staring at the yellow ceiling and the long line of little windows that looked like jail to me. My heart was pounding, like I'd just run a marathon. It wouldn't slow. It was in my throat all night long. And I was also terribly thirsty. In fact, it was another four weeks before I had to visit the bathroom for Number 2. I marveled at the whole process. My whole Flight did as well.

One of the Airmen was concerned. "I don't get it— why don't I need to take a shit?" he asked in some sort of Arkansas twang. "It's been days, yo. It's not natural?" The whole Flight was that way and we even started a pool of money, condoms and cigarettes to go to whichever guy was the first to have a verified, water-plopping bowel movement. It was a big deal. Guys went into the potties and strained to no avail.

Soldiers are an earthy sort. It doesn't really matter how cultured and sophisticated you are going in, once you're immersed in such a communal situation like Basic Training, things like pooping, peeing, farting, burping, masturbating, having sex, belch-talking and drinking take on a new meaning and importance. The funniest thing in the world became a juicy burp or a ripe fart ripped out of an Airman's butt, and, if it stank, that was a big plus. Our collective lack of pooping meant we were denied an old friend, and we carefully monitored the situation, wondering when our friend would return.

At about three and a half weeks in, a jubilant airman woke us all up. "Hey everybody, I just took a shit!" he cried. "Come look!" And we got up out of out racks and went into the head and were amazed.

Poop was there, and it was beautiful.

And, after that, Airmen started falling to the toilet gods like tenpins. My turn came about a week later. I'm pretty sure our communal lack of defecation was from being dehydrated, that our bodies began clinging to all the water it could. We also thought they (the TI's) were putting something in our food to prevent us from pooping—that was the rumor. We also thought they were putting saltpeter in our water to prevent us from becoming sexually aroused.

Airmen, if anything, are always ready to believe in a good conspiracy.

Dehydration, oh my God. I remember being so thirsty all the time, and you couldn't just go to a water fountain and get a drink like a civilized human being. You couldn't use the drinking fountain in the barracks because we would get in trouble for having a dirty, unserviceable fountain. So, I pursued water whenever I could get it. In the showers, I didn't wash, all I did was drink. In the chow hall I slurped down my two glasses of water that were mandatory on our trays and wanted more, though I was too chicken to leave the table and get it. And, yes, I even drank from the toilets because I didn't want to soil the water fountain which would be inspected by the TI's later.

Water, even from a toilet, was like liquid gold.

It wouldn't be for four weeks until my body settled and began behaving normally again and the roaring cry for water finally abated.

5
Suck, Bang, Blow

The ten weeks of training was divided into roughly five courses of two weeks in length, starting with basic engine operation and theory, the basic parts of the jet, and moving up toward actually laying hands on the engine itself and doing stuff to it.

My first class, a two-week course on basic engine theory, was located in a still operational part of White Hall in the Bermuda Triangle, the giant-sized building in the heart of the base. We were warned not to venture far from the classroom, as most of cavernous White Hall had been condemned and wasn't safe.

Mr. Carlson, the old ex-machinist civilian teaching the first course had a sure-fire method of vetting the students in his class. The first thing he did was make each of us read a few passages from our course material. His intention was to determine if we could read or not. Things were going fine until we got to the old Army Sarge wearing Staff Sergeant stripes. He leaned over his book, struggling and sputtering to sound things out. Mr. Carlson stopped him and led the guy from the classroom, and that was that.

Never saw him again. That seemed to be a common feature of military training, guys disappearing, never to be seen again.

A week and a half into the course, we were deep into it. The method in which jet engines work is really quite simple: air, sucked in to a cylinder, slowed and compressed to several atmospheres is then ignited and forced through a spinning turbine, which, in turn, drives the air compressor sucking in more air.

Or, put more crudely:

SUCK   BANG   BLOW

It's sort of like a perpetual motion device that requires air and fuel (therefore ruining the perpetual motion piece). The older jets, like the J-57 mounted in the B-52 warhorses, were turbojets, meaning they lacked a fan and ducted, bypass air. Newer ones, like the PW F110, were turbofans, using a great mass of ducted air to increase thrust. We also learned that American jets favored the Axial flow model using a combustion chamber, while British jets tended to be designed in a Centrifugal Flow with radial cans.

Our class leader, an old ex-Navy Sarge named Marseau, loved to tell us Air Force pukes how good we had it. He regaled us with Navy horror stories, from crumbling housing in squalid swamps to re-purposed, reheated food force-fed to the 'Squids' each day, he painted a dire picture. He was also big into the learning. "We got a big exam coming up, so instead of spending the entire weekend with your dicks in your hands, why don't you try cracking the books and studying up."

Being an old pro at taking tests from my Ohio State days, I didn't think too much of the course material. "But, Sarge," I replied, "me and my dick see so little of each other."

Lots of laughs. The test was easy.

One course down. Four more to go.

Most of our training from then on, was spent on learning how to maintain all the various things that are attached to the engine itself and imputing data into the dinosaur-like CAMS computer system the Air Force used for tracking parts. Many parts attached to the engine are held on by threaded bolts. The intense vibration of the jet engine necessitates the need to lock the various bolts in place via safety wire, otherwise they might untorque themselves during operation and come loose. Safety wiring was a big deal. You had to fish a piece of wire through a tiny hole in a nut or bolt. You then had to anchor the wire to another bolt or to a foundation in such a way that the wire forced the bolt to tighten instead of loosening. You had to apply a tight twist to the wire by means of a pair of specialized pliers. The final step was straightening the wire by giving it two good bangs with your pliers.

Bang! Bang!

I had the misfortune of working next to AB Mertz, who was a mountain-sized uncoordinated lug and general goof. I hated it when Mertz marched in the row behind me because he had a habit of climbing up my boots, scuffing them to high heaven, forcing me to get out my iron and cotton balls, heating up more shoe polish. Mertz was also a danger to everybody around him, which was usually me. They had a row of workstations set up where you could practice safety-wiring all you wanted. Of course, I was stuck on a station next to Mertz. Without looking what he was doing one day, he banged me right in the face with his stupid pliers.

I was understandably pissed. "Hey, Mertz, godammit, watch what you're …"

Bang! He got me with his pliers again, only this time right between the eyes. As I slumped to the floor and fell unconscious, I'm told I had time to call Mertz a "fucking idiot" just before everything went black. I don't really remember saying that, that's just what I was told I said.

The rest of our training was spent actually touching the engines, pulling off and reattaching the multitudes of parts attached to it. The facility we trained in was a formerly disused warehouse. The class was once conducted in the vast shops of White Hall, but had been moved as the base began its first transitioning steps toward closure.

The specter of base closure was rearing it head with greater frequency. I was starting to notice it more and more.

So, there it was, the Pratt & Whitney F100, the engine I was there to train on. The PW was a workhorse of the Air Force at the time, providing power for both the F-15 Eagle and the F-16. It was good experience, but, as I would come to learn, working on a dry engine mounted on a test rail in school was nothing like working on a real, wet one in the field. As Airman Mertz would put it, the ones at school were like an old, worn-out prostitute, with all the wrenches that had been turned on them over the years, all the parts were "loosy-goosy" and everything was all dried up. In the field, however, you were constantly covered with AV gas, toxic greases, asbestos, and other such hazardous things. The old

TF41 had blankets filled with asbestos that insulated tubing made of radioactive metal and lubed with carcinogenic grease. Also, the airplanes themselves were hard to work with. The old A7 Corsair II was a dream. You took the panels off with a speed handle and you had plenty of room inside. You could nearly stick your whole head and shoulders inside to work. The F16, on the other hand, was a whole different animal. The engine was tight in there—real tight, no room for anything. Many times you could barely see what you were doing. You'd reach in to do a job, and your hands would get hung up, wire and other sharp bits digging into your flesh and coating you with AV gas all at the same time. I once spent the entire afternoon with my hands hung up on the oil filter, the sharp ends of safety wire burrowed into my flesh, until my shop-mates came to save me.

That wasn't the only hazard. The engine was started by a giant capacitor that stored a large enough charge to kill a full-grown man if it wasn't properly grounded and discharged. Also, there was the noise, the infernal, screeching din the engine made when it was running, it would blast your ears, even with earplugs and defenders on. The vortex created by the motor made a little tornado out in front of the airplane that would suck in anything not bolted to the ground, you included.

Great fun.

As time passed, we got to know the members of other classes as we worked out in the bays. In one of our brother flights, an officer from the South Korean Air Force, was there on loan. As he was an officer, we initially gave him a wide berth, but, as time passed we got to know the guy and he was a decent fellow. I noticed he was missing a substantial part of his left middle finger, the first two knuckle joints were gone. I wondered and wondered what had happened to his finger.

Finally, one day, I asked. "What happened to your finger?"

And, he told me. While attending Andong National University, he was out with a group of angry students protesting a speaker who was delivering some bad news to the student population. Emotions were running high. The students were furious. Eventually, he became so mad at the speaker, he decided to demonstrate his displeasure by biting off his own middle finger and throwing it at the speaker. He had assumed the finger would be returned to him later for re-attachment, but, in the commotion, he never saw it again and had to endure the remainder of his life with a stubby digit.

What were the students protesting that caused such a passionate uproar? Apparently, the university had decided to cancel one of their student holidays, hence the contentious protest. I was truly impressed—to bite off one's own finger over a lost day off was certainly dedication.

6
Tiny Flag on the Wall

"Ping! Ping! Ping!"

A new batch of Pingers had arrived in the dayroom of the 42nd squadron, all wide-eyed in their blues freshly bounced off the bus. As they endured the barrage of 'Pings' I saw the distress in their eyes, the shocked bewilderment. They were used to being on top at Basic, now, here they were at Chanute, and getting hazed certainly wasn't something they had been expecting. One of the Pingers was a tanned, slender girl with shoulder-length whitish blonde hair leaking down out of her hat: LAMB, her name tag read. She was a 'Slick-Sleever', no chevrons, so she was an Airman Basic. She had bit of a rough-hewn Greek look to her, like a partially completed statue. Lamb pulled a wheeled, paisley print suitcase behind her.

Lamb, obviously tired after a long day of travelling up from Lackland and suddenly stuck in an unfamiliar and unfriendly place, looked like she was about to cry under the relentless assault.

I suddenly felt very sorry for Lamb. Being a college graduate, I was slightly older that the other trainees, who seemed rather predatory as they orbited around the pool tables. I was possibly a bit more mature than the rest, and I had no intention of hazing anybody. I felt it was my duty to try and save at least one of them and offer a proper welcome to Chanute, so I picked Lamb. I pulled her aside and offered her a chair. Smiling a little, she accepted and seated herself in a demure fashion.

"What's your name?" I asked.

"Lamb," she replied.

"I can see that. What's your first name?" After six weeks of using nothing but your last name, the opportunity to use your first name was a real treat.

"Ellie," she said in a small voice, brightening a little.

"Where you from, Ellie?"

"Galveston, Texas. What's 'Ping'?" she asked.

"Don't worry about it. After today you'll never hear it again."

I got Lamb a soda and helped cheer her up. I told her Chanute wasn't so bad. I don't know if she believed me or not.

"So, where are you from, Ren?" she asked, sipping her soda.

"Ohio, ever been there?"

"No, I'm sorry."

"I grew up in Ohio, but I was born in Texas. San Antonio."

That seemed to brighten her up. "Oh?" she said.

"Are you hungry? Have they shown you where the mess hall is yet?"

"No."

"Go get changed and I'll show you."

She glanced at her suitcase. "You mean, I can walk around in my normal clothes?"

"Sure. You're not at Basic anymore. This is tech school. It's off-hours."

Excited, Lamb found her dorm room and came back out in a pair of shorts, a tee-shirt and flip-flops. I took her to the 72nd squadron and Lamb had her first meal at Chanute.

And so began our strange, off-and-on relationship as fellow trainees at Chanute. I would see more of Airman Basic Ellie Lamb in the weeks to come, no longer a wide-eyed Pinger, she was like the Queen of Chanute, with the pick of an entire base full of horny young men at her call. Girls were an unusual commodity at Chanute, with the course-work mostly favoring men, males outnumbered females by at least twenty to one, if not more. A cute, modest girl like Ellie Lamb, who wasn't ugly and had no visible deformities, could have her way if she wanted to. I remember guys in the 42nd's dayroom lamenting over her, fighting over her. I remember every weekend she'd be hanging out with a different guy, even switching to the Navy at some point.

Ellie liked to call me and her the 'Texas Twosome'.

Texans tend to be proud of their state, and since I was from there originally, I earned a few bonus brownie points with her, two proud Texans representing at Chanute. Once from Texas, always from Texas, she thought. It was an odd thing with her, She'd hang out with me in the afternoons, but then move on to other guys just as quickly, as if the Texas Two-some part of her day was the nurturing PG-rated part, while other, more aggressive guys occupied the more steamy R and X-rated parts. Sometimes we'd plan to hit the chow hall or go to the BX, she'd excuse herself to go get something, but then never return. I wasn't overly interested in fostering any sort of romance and become embroiled in the fierce compe-tition that came with it, so I never consciously bothered to throw my hat into the ring—maybe that's what it was. Maybe Ellie wanted to see me getting my hands dirty, to actively fight for her. But, I never did. Sometimes, Ellie would help me save Pingers from hazing, and other times she would ac-tively Ping the newcomers. She was hard to figure out.

She was proud of her Texas heritage, and seemed to occasionally favor me because I was from Texas too. But, there was one small thing Ellie hadn't counted on. I had learned something. There comes a time in every young per-son's life when you are offered a moment of clarity. Mine came in the chow hall at Lackland AFB a few weeks earlier.

*   *   *   *   *

It was one or two weeks into Basic, when the ongo-ing campaign of psychological warfare waged against us was at its peak. I was standing there in the chow hall with my tray at an incomplete table, hungry, feeling low, tired of being yelled at, tired of being told I was crap all the time.

In the six week long carnival that is Basic Train-ing, the most danger-filled place you could possibly go is the chow hall. If you're going to get in trouble anywhere, that's where it's going to be. One would think the chow hall would be a welcome place of respite from all the gunk thrown at you day in and day out, a place to sit and eat and recharge your battery—but no. Quite the opposite, the chow hall was like the proverbial nectar-laden flower hiding a host of dangers where any wrong step could lead to your undoing. Each squadron had a detailed list of chow hall rules and regulations you had to follow—or else. None of these rules were written down anywhere, and if you asked to be orally briefed on them, silence would be your answer. You had to learn the rules the hard way, by screwing up, getting nicked, and getting called out for all to see. You had to stand in line a certain way. You had to be seated a certain way too. You also couldn't just take your tray, sit down and eat like normal people might. An assigned 'Table Guard' pointed to the table you had to sit down and eat from. Each table had four chairs facing north, south, east and west. To seat yourself, the first man had to move around the table counter-clockwise and stand behind the north chair. The second man would take the west chair, the third the south and the fourth the east. You had to stand there with your tray at the position of attention until the guy at the eastern chair said "Gentlemen, be seated." Then, and only then, were you allowed to sit down and eat. You could not be seated at a table that wasn't completely filled with Airmen. If you were unfortunate enough to find yourself at the end of the line, if your designated table wasn't filled, you could be standing there with your tray of uneaten food for a long time until another flight arrived. And, sometimes you got nothing, the TI's throwing you out after enough time had elapsed.

"Ummmmm, ummmm, good, ain't it? You're done, asshole. Get the fuck out!"

And, of course, like I said before, nobody tells you these rules—you find them out the hard way. It's like being in freakin' prison, everybody waiting to jump on you.

Another hazard of the chow hall was the dreaded Snake Pit. The Snake Pit was a long set of tables butted up against the wall where the TI's ate their meals. The Snake Pit was centrally located in the chow hall with a clear view of everything that went on, like the gods looking down at the doings of mortal men from Mt. Olympus. The TI's were ready and waiting to emerge from the Snake Pit at a moment's notice and pounce on any mistake in protocol, humiliating Air-

men with relish—the military's version of 'training'. If you
wanted ketchup, mustard, mayo, salt or pepper, a nice table
of all that was set up right in front of the Snake Pit—come
and get it, if you dare. To return your tray, you had to walk
the entire length of the Snake Pit to the blessed sanctuary of
the hopper, and then you had to perform an about-face and
cross the Snake Pit again to get out. Walking around, you
couldn't take a direct path to anywhere. You had to perform
a series of facing movements. You would march in one direction until you could march no further, then you would perform a right face or left face as the case may be and continue
marching until you reached another obstruction and you
would face again and so on until you reached your destina-
tion, the exit of the chow hall. To return your tray to the hopper, a soldier had to perform at least five facing movements,
each watched by the TI's. If you didn't do them right, if you
were slack, if you didn't take a good line, the TI's would be
all over you. (I recall once, as I was exiting the chow hall, I
saw AB Brad Pittman in quite a fix. Somehow, Pittman had
worked his way *behind* the damn Snake Pit and was trapped
between the table, a buttress, and the wall. There were no
TI's sitting there at the time. I saw him standing there next
to the buttress at the position of attention, no doubt trying to
puzzle out how he'd gotten there in the first place and, more
importantly, how he was going to get out. He performed an
about face and began marching his way out of peril. It was
a long march to get out of where he was. I thought he might
make it when, as I went out the door into the Texas sunshine,
I heard a ululation of screaming, several TI's appearing from
nowhere, proceeding to the Snake Pit with all speed to feast
on this unexpected and choice victim. Poor Pittman, all three
of his 341 demerits got pulled for that).

    If you were cue ball bald, if you didn't have a name
tag on your BDU's (the Pickled Relish guys as they were
called), then you were on the menu. The TI's even played
the "Hey you!" gag on the Relish guys, shouting it out to
see if anybody was dumb enough to stop. If you heard "Hey
You!" over your shoulder, you learned to just keep on walking—if the TI's really wanted you, they'd come and get in

your face—they weren't shy. Once you had a little hair, once you had your name tag on your BDU's, or 'Canned' as it was known, the TI's tended to leave you alone.

✶   ✶   ✶   ✶   ✶

So I was standing there with my tray waiting for more men to fill my table. I was feeling lonely and home-sick. I didn't want to be there anymore, and I felt like crying (I did more crying at Basic than I've ever done in my life, and I wasn't alone. Lots of big, tough guys, homesick and shell shocked, cried.) Behind the dreaded Snake Pit was a painted cinderblock wall mounted with the flags of all fifty states, and three more for Puerto Rico, Guam and the Virgin Islands. Texas' flag with its white-over-red stripes was mixed into the bunch.

The Texas Twosome, Ellie Lamb would one day refer to us as.

I grew up in western Ohio, but I wasn't born in Ohio. I was born in south Texas, in San Antonio in that odd estuary where American and Mexican cultures blend together. We were transplants, the first of our extended family to leave the beloved homeland, ever afterwards we were perpetual out-casts from afar. As a kid, I used my Texas heritage as a club. I loved to brag to all my Ohio-born friends during the doggy, allergy-riddled days of summer: "I'm not from here, pukes, I'm from Texas! Ha!" I said it with pride, I said it with vigor and thought such a distinction made me different and special from the rest. I thought I was too good to come from humble, lowly Ohio with its bugs and humidity and allergies.

The Texas Twosome...

But, years later, as I stood there in that squadron chow hall at Lackland Air Force Base waiting to sit down and eat, feeling as low as I've ever been, what did I see that lifted me up and gave me hope, gave me strength to keep plugging away? It wasn't the Texas flag.

I saw the little swallow-tailed Ohio flag, red, white and blue, mounted on the wall, mixed in with the rest, unique and bold. No mistaking the Ohio flag with its defiant pennant shape.

Ohio—where my family lived.

Ohio—where I went to school and grew up. An Ohio State graduate.

Ohio—

State flag of Ohio

where my one-day wife was born.

Ohio—a green land of safety and security never fully appreciated until that moment.

There comes a time in every person's life when you have a moment of clarity when all your fantasies are cast aside and you realize exactly who you are and where you come from. If you let that moment pass, if you don't understand the lesson being taught to you, then you are lost.

No more dreams of a big Texas sky. No more bluster. No more childhood delusions, for they mean nothing.

The little Ohio flag mixed-in with the rest.

I realized who I was.

I am a Buckeye, and I am from Ohio. Though Ellie Lamb probably couldn't imagine such a thing, I was born in Texas, but raised a Buckeye. There was no Texas left in my heart.

The table filled, I finally got to eat and, under the Ohio flag, I was nourished.

7

Green Street, the Squids and *Alien 3*

Six weeks in, I had the routine down. I took my classes, I did well. I stayed out of the MTM's way. I felt a sense of community, that I belonged there, could thrive there. I was now one of the 'Old Time Airmen' sitting in the dayroom in my half-BDU's like a saged Grand Poobah, the Pingers coming to me for comfort and advice. A call came down for a 'bad group of mother fuckers' to play volleyball against the hated 54th on Squadron Day. No longer hiding what I could do, eager to be a part of the action, I volunteered and demo'ed my skills for a drunken group of Airmen putting the team together. I made the 42nd volleyball team, no problem.

"We're going to pecker-slap those Jizz-bags in the 54th, right, Garcia?"

"Right!!"

"Let's fuck those fucking fuckers up!!"

I led the squadron formations, out in front as guide, wearing the little orange vest, setting the pace. Me and Matt Fujimoto (the guy from basic with the bag of junk food. He was there at the 72nd Squadron for turboprop school), started venturing out farther and farther from the safe area of our dorms. We started taking the civilian van service that went out to Green Street in nearby Champaign/Urbana on the weekends. Green Street is the equivalent of High Street at Ohio State, a long street skirting the university, populated with bars and other college hangouts. Matt and I weren't overly hardcore fellows looking to hang out in bars—drinking wasn't our thing. Once, at Basic, a Chaplain Colonel was giving us a fire and brimstone speech on the evils of heavy drinking. Matt was troubled, he interrupted the sermon with a question: "You don't mean water, do you?"

There was a cool arcade on Green Street where we liked to spend our quarters. One weekend, we shared the van back to the base with several Airmen, including Ellie Lamb

and her beau for the evening, AB Derrick Schotler, a pugna-
cious guy from New Jersey in my Jetmech class. Schotler
had been way over-served during his evening out with Lamb
and was stupid drunk. Ellie didn't seem impressed and spent
more time talking to me than her date.

The van driver in a red ball cap and black satin wind-
breaker eyeballed Schotler with suspicion. "Your friend back
there pukes in my van, there's going to be hell to pay, right?
I charge $300 bucks if I have to clean up puke."

As we wheeled our way to the base, Schotler turned
a lively shade of green—the inevitable was coming. Mt.
Schotler was soon to erupt. Ellie, perfumed and pretty in a
summer dress, scooted away from Schotler and sat to my
right, telling Fujimoto and me about her day.

The van stopped along the side of the road. "Is that
guy going to puke?" the driver wanted to know.

"Probably," I said.

"You fucking Airmen piss me off!"

I had heard this same driver earlier in the day, hands
in pockets, lamenting the fact the Airmen were soon going
away, along with a hefty portion of his business. The driver,
halted, pulled Schotler out of the van and made him kneel
over the ditch for several minutes.

Nothing happened. Schotler staggered back into the
van. Dubious, the driver continued. Soon we rolled up to the
main gate at Century Boulevard.

"Ellie…" he gurgled. And then …

"Oh hell no!" the driver cried, slamming on the
brakes. Everybody in the van jumped aside, Ellie lifted her
sandaled feet to avoid the giant pool of sick Schotler had
just made. The enraged driver and the gate SP (the Security
Police, or 'Sky Cops' as they were known) yanked him from
the van, had him on the ground and in handcuffs before you
could say the word 'boo', the driver screaming in his left ear,
the SP in his right.

"That's $300 bucks you owe me, asshole!" the driver
cried.

We dropped Matt Fujimoto off at the 72nd Squadron, then Ellie and I continued on to the 42nd. I felt really

close to her that night. If it wasn't for rules against PDA'ing (Public Displays of Affection) we probably would have held hands back to our dorm, it might have even been my turn to swap spit with her, as her date for the evening was under arrest back at the Century gate with the Sky Cops. She seemed willing.

But, no, we entered the dorm, got eyeballed by the CQ, and the moment was over. We wished each other good night.

That was the crazy thing about Ellie Lamb—on the verge of being close one second, cast aside the next.

I think that's when the Navy came into the picture. We'd see the sailors around the base, all of them taking a weather course in their unsightly dungarees, ironed-on stripes, stupid Swabbie hats and denim shirts. They didn't march like we did, rather they shambled down the road in a tangled mass, like some sort of Lovecraftian sea monster with multitudes of wiggling, unsynchronized legs. We didn't think much of the naval Squids, and they didn't think much of us, either. We'd hear them talking in the chow halls, how they hated 'girless', landlocked Chanute and how us 'Air Farce' bozos weren't real men when compared to them.

We were sitting in the chow hall for dinner. Ellie, still in her BDU's, came out with her tray. She saw me, waved, and headed in my direction. Even though attempts to hang out with Ellie usually ended in failure, like a Pavlovian Dog, I was excited at seeing her nevertheless. I liked Ellie, she was fun to talk to in those select moments when I had her to myself. About halfway to my table, a Navy guy with a cop mustache, hat in hand, intercepted her, making eyes and small talk. Before I knew it, Ellie sat down with the Squid and that was that—the Texas Twosome cut short again.

I was pretty much on my own that weekend, my usual companion, Matt Fujimoto, was stuck with extra-training for having failed a dorm room inspection—Fujimoto was a big fan of small metal boxes, he had a bunch of them decorating his room that he bought at the mall in Thomasboro and got busted for it. With little else to do, I decided to march out to the base theater a few blocks away to catch a flick. The theater was a standard military edifice: meager, outdated, with a crappy, over-priced concession stand, dark wood paneling galore and puffy vinyl seats in standard olive drab. It had one screen: a second-run copy of *Alien 3* was playing. I paid and went in, having to stand for the Star Spangled Banner first before the film rolled. This was my second time at the theater—the first time was with Fujimoto watching *Basic Instinct*. I remember not being able to hear a word of it, with the Airmen loudly baying at the screen during the numerous sex scenes. Watching a film at the base theater was like watching a rowdy midnight cult film.

Around halfway through, someone sat down in the seat next to me. Glancing over, it was Ellie, I could see her whitish blonde hair in the dark. In the half-light of the theater, I could also see her face was puffy, streaked with tears. I thought I saw her BDU shirt was slightly ripped. I don't know what happened to Ellie Lamb that evening and she never told me, but it was obviously traumatic. I raised my arm and she slid in, resting her head on my shoulder. We stayed that way for the rest of the film.

8
Those Marine Girls

After holding Ellie in my arms all evening, my dislike for the Navy reached an all-time high. The mustachioed Navy guy had assaulted Ellie and I wanted to make him pay, though I was never quite sure which one was the guy, I'd only had a fleeting glance at him in the chow hall, and Ellie wasn't talking. I'd look them over as they stumbled by, as if I were inspecting a lineup of suspected felons. I saw lots of guys who could have been him, but I was never certain.

The Navy, I couldn't stand them, the Marines too. There were several Naval groups assigned there taking various technical classes and a weather school for the Squids and Jarheads, and we resented everyone of them. They couldn't march, they were a bunch of pricks and they were also quite stupid, but we weren't allowed to pitch fun of them for it. It's easy to hurt the Navy's feelings.

But, despite my desire to tangle with a Navy guy and defend Ellie's honor, it wasn't with the Navy that I almost got into my one and only brawl while I was in the military, it was with the Marines stationed at the base.

Marine girls …

They were also there to attend weather school learning how to use, operate and take readings from metrological equipment. There was a brand spanking new weather school built across from the hangars near the old runway, and that's where they hung out.

The various services at Chanute tended to avoid each other, but, the base was only so big, therefore a pitched confrontation was inevitable. Every day, the Jetmechs, marooned at our distant shop on Eagle Drive, had to trudge down the street to go to the chow hall at P3. It was a long march—getting to anyplace was a long march at Chanute, the base had always been like that with trainees expected to pound out a lot of marching from one place to the next.

Once, the whole base revolved around massive, sunlit White Hall—you had classes there, you ate there, you even slept there too in the early days. When I got to Chanute, White Hall had already been mostly shut down and the schools, like ours, and the chow halls were scattered about. It was a whole lot of marching involved to get anywhere.

So we were marching to chow. There were about two hundred of us in two flights—the Aero Propulsion school being one of the larger ones on the base. We all had to carry our briefcases, which contained our school materials, pens and pencils, our books and raincoats. I was the guide. I enjoyed being the guide, wearing the little reflective vest and marching out in front, setting the pace. There we were, a squadron of two hundred Airmen marching in formation down the street to the chow hall at P3 with me leading the way. Coming down another street to my left was a platoon of about twenty-five Marine girls from the previously mentioned weather school. Even though our two differing branches wore similar BDU's (the old green Dog BDUs, not the cool computer-printed gray stuff they wear today), you could tell a Marine from a distance by their ribbed, peaked caps while Airmen's caps lacked the ribs and the peaks, like a painter's hat. They also had stripes while we had chevrons.

We had the right-of-way down the street, they were supposed to yield to us, and I was fully expecting our commander to give the order to make the turn to continue on.

The Marine girls, being marched being a typical neckless 'Jarhead' male, jumped in front and cut us off. We screeched to a messy, train-wreck halt as the Marines moved past, the squadron piling up behind me.

We grumbled.

They snickered and laughed.

"What's so funny?" I said, breaking protocol of silence while in the ranks.

They responded by making 'kissy' sounds and shaking their boobs. Their Jarhead leader called us a bunch of "… fucking Air Farce fuckheads."

"Fucky McFuckface, Air Farce!" one of them said.

Air Farce??? You don't say 'Air Farce' to Airmen.

No, no—not on our air base would they be permitted to call us names. Our commander said something back to the Jarhead. He halted his crew and they turned to face us, breaking ranks and rolling up their little sleeves.

"You want some, Air Farce?" one of them said to me, as I was out in front.

I tried to think of something witty to say in return, after all even back then I fancied myself a budding writer, certainly I could think up something cool and inventive to impress these Marine skanks with on the fly. "Fuck you!" I said after an internal struggle. I was struck with inspiration and I added "Bitch!" to my response. Very original.

The Marines stopped in the middle of the street and sized us up.

Of course, fighting with girls is not a noble pursuit, however, if you're going to do it, then do so with passion and without hesitation. My Air Force dander was up—I had been called 'Air Farce' and been disrespected on hallow ground, and I fully intended to beat the tar out of some Marine girl for it. We also outnumbered them ten to one, so they would have been destroyed in a brawl, no question.

I had a Marine girl all picked out, a little one with straw-colored hair who was doing a lot of trash-talking. I was going to throw my briefcase at her face and then bull rush the bimbo. I would sort out all the moral and ethical connotations of these fisticuffs later.

This was one damn beach the Marines were not going to take.

Air Farce my ass.

Just as we were ready to cleanse the Marines from the area with fist and boot, a full bird Colonel drove by in his staff car—the dreaded Colonel from the Bermuda Triangle who drove his Ford Escort around and was hard to spot. Brake lights and squeaky springs. He saw us milling about in a disorganized tangle and wanted to know "What the fuck was going on?" Our squadron leader and the Marine Jarhead gave him the lowdown through his rolled-down window. The next thing I knew, we were forming back up and watching the Marines march down the street.

Fight called off on account of a Colonel.

Ah well, I still fondly remember the little straw-haired Marine bitch I was going to throw my briefcase at and then beat the ever-loving dog piss out of. I wonder how she's doing today?

Such memories.

9
The Ether Bunny

The Ether Bunny was a legend floating around the dorms and dark spaces of Chanute. He might have been a fixture of other bases as well, and possibly of various college campuses—any place where young men with impressionable minds congregated and were off on their own, the Ether Bunny might be lurking about. As a 'Pinger' at Chanute, I got to know all about him and his various sinister habits told to me by snickering Airmen in the day room and the chow halls.

"Don't go to the chow hall after dark by yourself—the Ether Bunny will get you!"

"Watch out for the base theater. If you go see a film, and you notice that somebody's sitting next to you who wasn't there before, might be the Ether Bunny."

"Listen for the sound of a can rattling across the ground...that's him."

"See that alley over there?? The Ether Bunny fucked some poor guy down in there. Hard!"

The Ether Bunny was the 'Boogie Man' of Chanute, ever present in the tight corridors and confining rooms of the dormitories. In the pre-dawn before the proliferation of the internet in 1992, you didn't have the web surfing, smart phones and DVDs. TV's were scarce and libraries out of fashion, so you had stories and whispered rumors direct from people's mouths to entertain you, and, usually, it was the most lurid and sinister of stories that captured one's thoughts and lingered. It was the Time of the Ether Bunny, and he reigned supreme as a dark specter of Airmen's psychedelic, sex-tinged fantasies.

The story of the Ether Bunny, in its most basic form, was as thus: he was a depraved person, either a trainee or a lowly civilian staff member who preyed upon lone men with a rag saturated with ether with the intent of knocking out and raping that person. He could pop up anywhere, and one should certainly never walk alone or you might wake up hours later missing something. The story was silly and quite old from a time long gone. Certainly, I wouldn't think a mad pervert on the prowl would want to make use of a volatile, hard-to-transport and flammable dose of ether as his anesthesia of choice. In our modern world an innocuous pill dropped into a drink would do much better, but, for shock value, the Ether Bunny and his dented up, dingy can of ether did quite well.

The Ether Bunny was changeable, moldable, multipurpose Boogie Man. In some tellings, he was a 'she', a demented female from some backwater part of the country hoping to sodomize a lone man as payback for mistreatment she'd received at home. In other tellings, the Ether Bunny wasn't a single person but a cult of people with a hidden meeting place located somewhere in the craggy old buildings of Chanute. The story even went that you could see their hidden courtyard from the air littered with the detritus and accessories of their bizarre rituals and that they had, through some sort of off-base influence, forbidden airplanes from flying overhead as they might look down from above and witness their activities.

Ellie Lamb certainly believed in the Ether Bunny.

Even I, with my clear, empirical, college-educated mind, wasn't immune to his allure. I remember one evening I was studying for an exam and was quite tired. Ellie Lamb was there in her usual tee-shirt, shorts and flip-flops. She was a few weeks behind me, and I was helping her cram for an exam. Whenever she needed help with her coursework, she would turn to me, and the Texas Twosome was back on. It was getting late, females weren't supposed to be alone in a male's dorm room at such hours—getting caught by an MTM or a rope would mean huge trouble. Ellie gathered her things, put her flip-flops back on and exited. Her room was on the other side of the dorm, so she had a far ways to walk.

I quickly heard a frantic knock on my door. "Ren, Ren, let me in!"

It was Ellie, wide-eyed like she was back on her first day getting Pinged. She scooted in and shut the door.

She composed herself. "I saw this creepy guy, standing at the end of the hall. He really scared me. I saw a beat up old can in his pocket. Ren, what if he's the Ether Bunny?"

"There is no Ether Bunny," I said. "Just a tall tale."

"Go out there and look!" she insisted.

I went out into the brightly lit hallway and saw nothing, just a long, empty corridor with a perfectly polished floor, dotted with a series of orderly closed doors. I decided to hit the latrine one last time before bed and tell Ellie to stop being a baby. While I was in there performing my business, I recall smelling something, a rotten sort of smell. I figured a pipe must be backed up somewhere.

When I came out, I wasn't alone. I saw, standing a fair distance away at the end of the hallway, a janitor I didn't recognize. You'd see janitors every so often, usually in the mornings always busy doing something. I remember this janitor wasn't working, just standing there in his rumpled clothes staring at me.

I remember seeing a beaten-up white can of some sort sticking out of his pocket, just like what Ellie had described.

I hurried back to my room and locked the door behind me. Ellie was sitting on the bed. "Did you see him?" she asked.

"I saw somebody, just a janitor."

Ellie looked a little frantic. "Ren, I don't want to walk back to my room. Can I stay here tonight? We won't get caught, I promise. There aren't any MTM's around today."

"What about the ropes?"

"I know all the ropes. They won't come knocking."

I thought about it. I figured she was right—the MTM's were all busy figuring out what other assignments they could get before the base shutdown, their presence around the squadron dorm had become rather scarce as of late. I agreed, as I didn't have a roomie at the time. I set her up in the other bed—such a gentleman I was. She pulled loose the scratchy green blanket and crawled in.

"Thanks, Ren," she said, settling in, springs fussing.

A short time later, I heard a rattle outside in the hallway, followed by a knock at the door. I could see the shadow of somebody standing there through the light of the door crack. Blistering thoughts of MTM's or ropes crossed my mind. I was sure we were getting caught, getting hauled out of my room. The demerits, the washing back and possible time spent in CC. The snickers from my classmates.

There was something sinister about the knock I heard. A knock from an MTM would be forceful and profane, *"Open the fucking door!"* This knock was slow and quiet. A horror movie knock.

Springs rattled, feet pattered across the floor. Before I knew it, Ellie was in my bed with me. "Who's at the door?" she asked.

"Don't know."

"Don't answer it." We clung to each other in the bed, Ellie still in her tee shirt, but having shed her shorts.

"Oh, God," she said, whispering, her mouth close to mine. "You smell that?"

Sure enough, I thought I smelt something strong, like peroxide, that made my nose burn.

I also thought I saw the doorknob being tried from the other side. Me and Ellie held onto each other through all this. I could feel the contours of her butt through her underwear and she pressed the soles of her feet against my shins. Minutes later Ellie was fast asleep, and I soon followed. We forgot all about the Ether Bunny on the other side of the door. Of course nobody came through and we probably just imagined the whole thing. I often wonder what Ellie thought about that night? Was I supposed to make a pass at her? Were we supposed to have sex? Did she think any less of me that she spent the night in my bed and nothing happened?

In the morning, Ellie was gone, back to her room. I had a rotten headache, and I remember clearly smelling peroxide at my door.

Maybe Ellie Lamb was the Ether Bunny?

Remember Me

The first few snowflakes of Chanute's Fimbul Winter began to fall about week four of my time there.

Though the base would operate for another year or so, it felt like the end was near. The MTM's made no further pretense of managing our military training, they were busy looking for soft places to land within the Air Force. Our teachers lamented the whole thing. They spoke of either retirement or change of career. Our training began to feel rather by-the-numbers as the Aero-Propulsion school readied to be moved to Sheppard.

Potential suitors to take over the base came and went. What was under Chanute was also a source of stories and speculation. It was long known that Chanute was an environmental disaster. Generations of AV gas, of chemicals, toxic greases, asbestos, furans, and industrial waste were sealed up into metal drums and either stored in ill-suited warehouses or, worse, buried on the base plowed-over with dirt from a bulldozer. The Heritage Lake area at the southern frontier was supposed to be especially bad and we were warned not to swim there. "Might come out glowin'!" they told us. And, indeed, in 2000, Heritage Lake on base was declared an EPA Superfund site for all the bad stuff that was stored and buried there.

All that mess was supposedly what held up the sale of the base to the Dalai Lama. It was a persistent rumor that the Dahli Lahma wanted to buy the base and start 'digging into the ground.' Should he have done that, he might have dug into a cache of leaking, buried barrels from the `50's containing who knows what.

A song played on the radio, "*Don't be Cruel to Rantoul ...*", a play on an Elvis song.

As I walked the clean, sun-washed streets littered with old planes and military monuments, I wondered what would happen to the base I now felt at one with. I quickly learned to love the place, the old bricks and the friends I'd made. I'd spent Basic trying to hurry up and get it over with. I remember my favorite marching song matched my mood:

Oh, I want to go home,
But they won't let me go home ...
They say that in the Air Force, the pay is mighty fine.
They give you a hundred dollars, and take back ninety-
nine...
Oh, I want to go home,
But they won't let me go home ...
They say that in the Air Force, the food is mighty fine.
The chicken jumped off the table and killed a friend of
mine...
Oh, I want to go home,
But they won't let me go home ...
They say that in the Air Force, the chicks are mighty fine.
They look like Godzilla and walk like Frankenstein ...
Oh, I want to go home,
But they won't let me go home ...

But now, I really didn't want to go home. I'd just arrived, and the end for Chanute was near. The loss I felt.

I remember once seeing a small plaque on Western Ave in Cincinnati.

SITE OF CROSLEY FIELD
ON THIS SITE, BOUNDED BY WESTERN AVENUE TO THE EAST,
FINDLAY STREET TO THE SOUTH, AND YORK STREET TO THE NORTH,
THE CINCINNATI REDS PLAYED BASEBALL FROM 1884 TO 1970

Crosley Field, the old home of the Reds prior to the Concrete Jungle of Riverfront Stadium, had been gone for all but first three years of my life, yet I felt its loss, hankered for the old wooden bleachers crammed into the decaying Western Avenue environs, the drifting smell of popcorn and tobacco, and the crack of the bat. Ghosts at the fallen turnstiles.

    And now, there I was, mourning Chanute. The place wasn't even finished yet and I felt its passing. I imagined a similar plaque tacked onto White Hall:

HERE WAS CHANUTE AIR FORCE BASE
TAUGHT MANY STUDENTS
FROM 1917 TO 1993

    I wondered. Did I place too much value on things and places long gone? What is a place but something that comes and goes?

    I had hopes that Chanute wouldn't fall away and become a ruin. The city of Rantoul, isolated and quite dependant on Chanute for its existence, seemed confident that it would be 'all right' without the old base to support it. I thought about the van drivers taking me and Matt Fujimoto to Green Street every weekend, cleaning up Schotler's puke afterwards. What would happen to them? Who would they have to drive around?

*   *   *   *   *

    Graduation day. Time to leave Chanute and go home, back to the green valleys of Ohio.

    As I packed, I noticed a note written on a folded scrap of paper sat innocently by my door.

> *Before you go, please come see me.*
> *I want to tell you something.*
> *—Ellie*

    Ellie Lamb had left me a note under my door. We'd had a touch and go seven weeks together since she'd arrived and I'd saved her from getting 'Pinged' in the dayroom. We always had fun when we ate or studied together, but those were just fleeting moments. She'd become intoxicated by the attention she was receiving, all those female-starved Airmen lined up at her door. She'd given me a few opportunities to toss my hat in, to make my case for her, as on the shuttle bus coming from Green Street, but things had never seemed to work out. I'd wait too long and some other guy would win her hand for the night, then, that Saturday when things seemed to be clicking and we might hook up, Schotler pukes all over the floor of the bus and spoils the mood. Then there were the blackened eyes at the movie theater and the Ether Bunny incident where we didn't have sex.

There was always something with Ellie.

But, perhaps just as I'd matured into a better wiser person ready to tackle the rest of my life, perhaps Ellie had too. Maybe she was tired of the situation, grocery shopping for Airmen each and every day, and was looking for a change of pace.

I want to tell you something...

Whatever the case, I never found out what she wanted to tell me. Graduation day had come and gone, my folks arrived and took me away from Chanute back to Ohio. I never saw or heard from Airman Basic Ellie Lamb again. All sorts of things swirled around in my head. I wonder why I didn't seek her out before I left? I think, maybe, I wanted her to feel what it was like to be left holding the bag, to be abandoned, to get her hopes up, and then get nothing.

Maybe all she wanted to say was thanks for everything and good luck, have a nice life.

Maybe she wanted to tell me something more—something profound. Maybe me just up and leaving like I did hurt her badly. Who knows?

Years later, I tried to find her, looking on facebook and the like, but I have yet to be successful. I sometimes wonder, wherever she is, if she looks back at her days at Chanute with fond nostalgia and thinks of me, just as I often think of her.

Maybe …

11
In Ruins

I came back to Chanute about twenty years later in 2012. I don't really know why I went, something deep inside just called me there. Alone, I took the long drive west across Indiana into the flatlands of Illinois.

I knew the base had been closed for some time, but I don't think I was prepared to see what awaited me as I rolled up Century Boulevard from the south, the road slick from a sudden afternoon storm common in the Mid-West. In 1992, with Chanute surrounded by standard chain link fencing topped with barbed wire, access to the base was limited to only a few points. Closure hadn't fully registered in my head. I expected things to be pretty much like how I remembered it—closed, but still locked up tight as it had been. I thought I'd have to enter through the Main Gate at Route 45 and Century and roll south into the main part of the base. How else would I get in?

Like biblical Jericho, all the fences were taken down. All the formerly restricted areas of the base once limited in access to only a select few, were wide open to the barbarians. I just kept driving and there I was rolling unhindered through formerly hallowed ground.

There was a large white plane with four propeller engines parked near Century Boulevard at the southern reaches of the base. It looked to be a C-97, a post WWII B-29 modification. I would have guessed all of the ceremonial aircraft once dotting the base would be gone, moved onto other bases. I wondered why the plane was still there sitting by itself at the edge of a field as I drove past it.

The place didn't look familiar to me as I turned onto Enterprise Drive. I usually have a pretty decent sense of direction, but, the years had taken their toll on my memory and nothing that I saw was as I remembered it to be. It was like visiting your old hometown after years of being away and

The "White Plane" parked in a field off of Century Boulevard
(C-97). Picture taken by the author in 2016, after the closure of the
Chanute Aerospace Museum. The rudder and tail plane have been
removed. (RDG)

seeing it different, seeing it fallen into disrepair. The streets
were empty, the asphalt cracked, wispy with grass and tough
weeds peeking through. The sidewalks were uneven and
bumpy. The buildings huddled along the roadside, bleached
and discolored after years of neglect, were ominously still.
The trees dotting the curbside looked like they belonged in
a boot hill cemetery. Occasionally I'd catch a hint of slight
movement only to find an ajar door swinging in the wind.
Coming up Enterprise Drive, there was a pervasive, abrupt,
vacated feel, as if there had been a nuclear tragedy and everyone had been evacuated on the spot where they stood and
moved out fast, never to return.

In my days there, traffic moving up and down the
streets would be halted in the morning to allow the Airmen
to march to class. Today, there was no traffic at all. I stood
in the middle of the street for a long time. Nobody drove by.

Could this be the resplendent place so full of life I
remembered so fondly? Echoes of old voices passed across
my head as I wallowed in the silence and decay.

"Fly, fight and win!!"
"Chanute!!"

But, that's all they were, just echoes.

I continued down Borman into the old Bermuda Tri

Enterprise Drive, facing north. Faktor Hall, the old 72nd squadron, where Matt Fujimoto lived, can be seen in the distance. The 42nd (not in the frame) is to the left. The street was crumbling, devoid of traffic in 2012. (RDG)

angle, the bleeding heart of the base where Airmen trainees like myself once feared to tread.

I passed a sizable weedy patch of grass. The parade grounds! I remember, where we marched in our blues before an appreciative crowd, all of us carrying a state flag. A B-58 Hustler, a very photogenic supersonic bomber from the 1960's, used to watch over the parade grounds from its ceremonial pad.

The Hustler was gone, the grounds turned into a wild, unrestrained meadow. I wondered again why the white plane was still there near Century.

It hit me. I knew why: *nobody wanted it.*

Moving on, there was the stern and imposing Base HQ in fortress-like brown brick along with a few homes running down Arends Boulevard—homes high-ranking officers and their families used to live in. Some of the homes looked occupied. The lawns needed mowing and perhaps a bit of landscaping. A touch of paint would have been nice too. Children's toys lay out in the grass. A car on blocks rusted in

Above: Chanute's noir Base HQ in the heart of the Bermuda Triangle, overgrown with trees in 2012.

Below: The rear of the HQ, also heavily overgrown with trees. (RDG)

one of the driveways. The trees in front of the old HQ were out of control, their branches knocking into the sides of the building, obscuring it from view. Some of the windows were cracked. Inside the main entrance was a hobo's detritus of dirty sheets, a thrown mattress and a muddy bicycle. The place had a singularly vacant sort of feel. Behind HQ was a small park featuring an abstract statue dedicated to training and learning. The grass was weedy and unkempt. The flag pole, once attended to with precision and reverence every day, was without a flag. Graffiti was scratched into its metal grain surface.

Down the street was the Base Hospital, a rather gothic-looking place more suited to stormy skies in an atmospheric horror-themed video game than a run-down street.

More of the same: weeds, cracked windows, suffering from a dearth of love and attention; a FOR SALE sign in hand-painted red letters was nailed askew to a heavy-growth tree

Looming not far away down Commerce Drive was the grand sprawl of the P3 building, or White Hall as it was later called. White Hall was once the largest multipurpose building in the US Military, not surpassed until the construction of the Pentagon in 1943. With its long, unrelenting façade and multiple courtyards, White Hall looked like a harp or a long bow from the air, take your pick. In its day, White Hall was referred to as 'Buckingham Palace' for nothing else like it existed in the military at the time. It contained classrooms, dorms, shops, soda fountains, gymnasiums, the works; a thriving city within itself.

White Hall was a special place, the crown jewel of Chanute. I myself had studied and eaten at White Hall and never knew it because the place was so large and sprawling.

Now, it was a long, morgue-like edifice, like a can full of horror film yet to be shot. Trees, loaded with dead runs and looking like they'd been stripped bare and twisted up by a tornado, dotted Commerce Drive in front of White Hall

The giant White Hall, once the crown jewel and heart of Chanute, a disfigured, haunted hulk in 2012. A chemical process known as efflorescence where salts in the bricks migrate to the surface, literally turn it white. (RDG)

like a chorus of deformed demons. The building itself, once a uniform shade of suburban brown in perfectly laid bricks, was an unsightly, splotchy mess, the bricks themselves vomiting out minerals from within and literally turning the building white. It looked like a stricken human being on the verge of transforming into a flesh-eating zombie. It lay astride the length of Commerce Drive like the corpse of a

great behemoth, rotting and spoiled, but far too tough to fully fade away. The courtyards were blocked by rotting wooden fences half-heartedly held shut with rusting chains. Looking inside, they were overgrown with trees punched up through the concrete. A pile of worn tires near a junked AV-gas truck and an observation tower of rusted struts all looked spectacularly unsafe.

Peering into the windows was a scene out of an apocalyptic disaster movie. Fallen plaster, caved-in metal, shattered glass, peeling paint, satanic graffiti, defaced murals, standing water: the interior was a sight right out of hell itself. The overhang at the main doors looked on the verge of falling in. Water dripped into stagnant pools. I could smell the accumulation of mold even from the outside.

A guy in a truck drove by and stopped. Eyeballing me, he wanted to know what I was doing there. Told him I was just taking pictures, even showed him my camera. He told me the building was not safe. Lots of 'bad people' were inside. Cops wouldn't even go in there, he added. The building was slated to be torn down, but had been delayed for twenty years due to the volume of asbestos and mold inside. A stay of execution for this once grand place.

I got back in my car and continued past Pacesetter

Hangar 2, once converted into a sporting arena to host boxing matches, looked like a pagan temple in 2012 (RDG)

Drive and the row of hangars into the tarmac and runways. I could have driven out into the runway if I wanted and nobody would have stopped me. A golf course loomed ahead to the northeast. In the afternoon silence, I could hear the distant roar of lawnmowers attending to the greens. The old firehouse in front of the base water tower was sealed up tight. The hangars were lonely and sad, like a set of cast aside tin cans. There was activity near the southern-most hanger. I saw cars parked and a motley collection of aircraft pushed close together. The hanger had been repurposed as an aerospace museum. At least there was some activity going on. Opposite the hangar, the weather school had been occupied—the logo for AT&T hung from the tower.

I mounted back up and headed south on Eagle Drive, looking for something familiar. Near a disused concourse I saw the old warehouse on the corner of Flessner and Eagle where I took most of my Jetmech classes—I recognized the windowless, silvery metal walls giving it a space-age sort of look. That building seemed pretty much as I remembered it. Seeing the old Jetshop got things going, it was all coming back to me.

The Base Theater, a place I once spent a lot of time in, a weed-infested tomb locked up tight in 2016 (RDG)

Continuing west on Neal Drive, I passed a red mausoleum-like structure on the right presiding over a pad of cracked concrete and furry trees. I stopped. I knew this building, it was the tiny base theater, a wonderland of red bricks where I watched *Basic Instinct* with Matt Fujimoto and a bunch of unruly Airmen, and where I comforted Ellie Lamb in the dark while watching *Alien3.* The roof had partially fallen in, the theater seats exposed to the elements, rather like how Ellie had been that evening: open, broken, laid bare.

I got back in my car, headed west on Neal for a few blocks and turned right on Enterprise. The years were erased, here I was, back in the student safe area where I lived for 10 weeks. I drove past the hated 54th. The 54th had new life, having been re-purposed as some sort of home for troubled youths. A few blocks north past the broad grassy spaces lining the street was my old dorm, the 42nd sitting on the green like a rectangular garnet. Unlike the reborn 54th, it was dead. Driving up, it was an abandoned relic. Like White Hall, the two central courtyards where me and my fellow Jetmechs once gloriously marched in to thunderous cheers every afternoon, were overgrown with scrubby brush and trees. I waded in, hot, steamy, Congo-like, until I got to the locked up dayroom in the center, the tinted windows soaked in silence. I saw hints of tables and chairs tossed about inside. I could still imagine Ellie Lamb walking into those locked doors with her suitcase, getting Pinged by a host of jeering ghost voices.

Her note passed through my head: *I want to tell you something...*

Looking around, the glossy windows bowed in the afternoon heat. A jungle-like vine had invaded a gutter and torn it away from the building. I exited the courtyard.

Around the corner was the main entrance: double doors with Gates Hall in clean metal letters partially obscured by tree branches. I remember once charging out those

Gates Hall, main entrance to the 42nd Squadron.

doors in my tee shirt and gym shorts with black socks and my Lackland low-riders as we sped off to do battle with the 54th at a vicious game of no-rules volleyball during Squadron Day. *"Gentlemen, we've an emasculation of louts to handle!"* I once shouted. I remember Ellie Lamb, watching, cheering me on as we played. I remember showing off for her, throwing my body around the grassy court as we beat the 54th.

Now, the lobby inside the locked doors was a mess. Wreckage scattered everywhere. The old CQ desk, an ugly metal contraption, was still there, turned backwards, stuff piled up on it. I could see the narrow corridor to the left, that went down a ways, took a hard right and went past my old

dorm room.

The squadron logo, the THUNDERING 42nd, draped with red lightning bolts, was painted on the wall, unfaded with time along with the phrase: COMMITMENT TO EXELLENCE.

Here I studied, slept, laughed, learned to be a soldier, and a man too.

Who I am today was bequeathed to me here. The aimless boy I was still wanders these halls.

Desolation and strewn wreckage.

Abandoned, just like the plane off of Century.

Nobody wanted it. Nobody cared.

Well, I cared. This place meant something to me.

My heart broke.

Ghosts of the Past

At lot has happened since I was last there in 2012. Many of the base buildings have either been occupied by various civic and local private organizations, or they've been torn down. The things that made Chanute are slowly disappearing, fading into just another part of Rantoul.

Site of the former 42nd Squadron on the corner of Enterprise and Borman Drives in 2016. The 42nd has been replaced by a cluster of new dormitories built by the State of Illinois. (RDG)

The tormented shell of the 42nd is gone. If you go to the corner of Borman and Enterprise today, you'll see the State of Illinois is busy throwing up a complex of butt-ugly housing where the 42nd used to be. The missile looming over the old gate at Liberty and Borman is still there on an island of grass, presiding over a crumbling street people rarely drive down.

After many delays, White Hall is finally demolished. I visited Chanute in July, 2016. Pacesetter Drive was closed. A bumpy construction fence had been thrown up. Bulldozers smoothed the ground once inhabited by White Hall, leaving a vast open space. Many wished it would have stayed, looming over Commerce Drive like fossilized Noah's Ark, as it

View from Pacesetter Drive looking west toward Arends Boulevard in 2016. White Hall, the great jewel of Chanute since the 1930's, has been demolished, leaving a massive empty spot scraped clean. (RDG)

had since the `30's. It was a glorious building, even in its sunset. Several paranormal and ghost-hunting groups claim White Hall should have been preserved as one of the most haunted sites in Illinois, making it a rather demented sort of Disneyland for the ghost-hunter. Anybody with sense can see the place was haunted just by looking at it. Now that it's gone, a vast green space is planned to take its place. Even the ghosts have vacated.

The white plane is still there, overlooking a green field off of Century Boulevard, its tail plane dismantled. It overlooks a small road heading to the Chanute Aerospace Museum which had taken up residence in Grissom Hall, the southern-most hanger. As of November, 2015, the museum is closed. The Village of Rantoul, which had been subsidizing its existence for a number of years, could no longer afford the cost. The museum was an amazing place, celebrating the rich history of Chanute. Now, it's a vacant shell, just like the base itself.

*   *   *   *   *

So passes Chanute, a place of wonder, the American

Timbuktu, slowly being assimilated by a tiny village in Illinois or being torn down.

That hallowed ground I trod upon, appreciated by a scant few. I appreciate it. My heart is still there. As a 25 year old boy, Chanute was what I needed. Without it, who would I be?

My wife often accuses me of having a chronic case of over-sentimentality, that I place too much value on places and things that don't deserve such love. I feel the same way about Ohio State too, another one of my old haunts. She went to Eastern Kentucky University, and couldn't care less about it.

"Feel like driving down to EKU and have a look?" I sometimes ask her.

"Why?" is her usual response. I suppose she's right, I am a sentimental person, but I think that's a good thing, to fondly remember the places that helped forge me as a complete person, even if they're long gone.

I still think about Ellie Lamb—she was a person I could have cherished, she could have been Mrs. Garcia, had the chips fallen correctly. Just like Chanute, she no longer exists. I sometimes fill-in what she wanted to tell me on that final day before I left with my own musings. Any more, I hear her voice in my ear, whispering:

Let me go...

What other choice do I have? I'm married now, with a house, a job and a bunch of dogs. Both Ellie and Chanute have passed into memory—things I loved that can no longer be. Still, in my dying days, when I pass to the earth just as Chanute has, I will hear those stirring words chiseled in the stone of my memory:

"Fly, Fight and Win!"
"Chanute!"

Fin
RDG—Feb 2016

Expanded Content

The Razor Incident

After getting some initial feedback for my little military epic, *10 Weeks at Chanute,* it appears people really want to know more about the crazy 'razor incident' I briefly mention in Chapter 4 that happened to me at Basic Training—the part where I had to write sentences discussing my incompetence as an Airman, or else. That was a pretty big to-do, actually.

"What happened, what happened?" people ask.

I have, literally, tons of humorous anecdotes from my time in the service, and, for the sake of brevity and flow, I had to leave most of them out so that the story wouldn't stall. Most of these assorted tales take a fair amount of time to set-up to properly describe, and I didn't want to bog down the flow of the narrative in pointless minutia, so I left them out which is sad because most of these little side stories are truly funny. They're tales good for an old-fashioned Bull Session at the bars, at cocktail parties or church socials. Armed with stories like these you're sure to be a big hit.

But, the Razor Incident seems to have piqued a good measure of interest, so I decided to throw it in here at the back of the book as sort of an 'optional' bit of reading.

Ok, you want to know, so I'll tell you.

The Razor Incident…

* * * * *

Aside from the deadly Chow Hall, a very perilous task at Basic Training is having to perform Dorm Guard duty. Most everybody has to do it at some point during the tour, and you just have to pray that it doesn't get you in mounds of trouble—because it certainly can.

Essentially, the Dorm Guard does just that—guards the door to the dormitory. For three hours you had to stand there in a little cubbyhole by the door wearing your hat and a web belt, and monitor all those wishing to enter the dorm and all those wishing to exit the dorm. The Dorm Guard was the only person allowed to touch the handle to the door—all others were forbidden to touch it. If somebody outside pounded on the door, you had to peer through the narrow window, see who it was, and check a sheet with a list of names to see if that person was authorized to enter or not. If they were on the list, then you could open the door. If it was a female, you had to shout "LADY ENTERING THE DORM!"

If the person was not on the list, then you were not supposed to let them in, no matter who it was.

Being the Dorm Guard was mighty dangerous, as the MTI's loved to screw with them. They would intentionally send TI's not on the authorized list to the door to see if they could prod the poor, stressed-out Dorm Guard into letting them in. They would pound on the door, stand there, scream at the Dorm Guard, threaten them, the whole nine yards, hoping to stress them into opening the door.

And, if the Dorm Guard yielded to the pressure, that was it—they would get recycled. Washed back. Almost immediately.

Yeah, it sucked.

Obviously, being the Dorm Guard was something you didn't want to do. A brother Airmen would get assigned the duty of scheduling the Dorm Guard rotations, and therefore, that was a guy you wanted to be friends with so you could get the more plum Dorm Guard assignments, like, say, in the middle of the night when the TI's were less-likely to come to the door. But, no matter what time of day or night, trouble could always find you if you were stuck standing there by the cubby hole.

* * * * *

So, it was 9:00pm, time for lights out at glorious Lackland Air Force Base. 9:00pm sounds pretty early in the evening, and it is, but, after a long day of marching and getting yelled at, you were usually pretty tired. With no napping allowed during the day, even a night owl like me was always ready hit the sack at 9:00pm.

But, the unthinkable had happened and I was on the rotation to be Dorm Guard, a shift lasting three hours—which always seemed like an eternity. So, instead of getting into my skivvies for sleep, I had to put on my hat, grab a flashlight and my BMTS Training Manual and take over for the previous guy. Me and the Dorm Guard I was relieving would then have to walk the bays, checking for any items that would be potentially unsafe or be considered CONTRABAND.

Contraband was easy to classify: Contraband was:

Drugs
Alcohol
Cigarettes
Weapons
Women

In walking the dorm, we didn't find any contraband, obviously; just a dorm full of guys getting ready for bed. We had a Sister Flight in the dorm behind ours and they liked to pass us notes under the common door in the day room. Some of the guys were flopped on their racks, all grins, busy penning or reading love letters to their girlfriends on the other side—girls they'd never actually seen, other than as passing shadows drifting through the bottom of the door and as alluring half-heard giggles. We made the would-be Casanovas wrap it up and hit the sack, which they did.

As we finished the walk through, I spied an innocuous electric razor plugged into a wall outlet, a red light blinking as it charged.

An electric razor plugged into the wall? Big deal, right?

Wrong.

Everything's big deal at Basic.

We weren't allowed to have facial hair at all at Basic, not even the Five-O-Clock shadow. You had to be totally clean-shaven at all times.

"Garcia, you fuckin' butcher, what is that shit all over your face?" the TI's would ask all the time.

So, we were shaving constantly, every spare moment we had, mostly with cheap disposable razors bought a hard march away at the BX. Aside from shining our boots, shaving our faces took up most of our time. As such, our faces were scraped raw, so much so many of us were afflicted with

Pseudofolliculitis Barbae, the dreaded 'shaving disease', our faces, usually around the chin area, covered with tiny pimple-like bumps that hurt like living hell. Through the scuttlebutt, I had heard one Airman in our dorm had brought an electric razor with him to Basic, which wasn't against regulations, but was a tangible focus for the TI's to hate on should they see it. They wanted us disfiguring our faces with the cheap disposable stuff.

And there it was, the razor happily blinking on the wall, plugged in, charging up. I figured the razor probably shouldn't be there, but didn't say anything—I figured the owner would hide it in his locker before lights out anyway.

I took the web belt, put my hat on and assumed the position in the cubby hole, seeing the ominous sign hung over it reading in lurid red letters: STAY ALERT! I clearly remember hallucinating one dark night, the letters on the sign transforming before my eyes to read: STAY THE FUCK ALERT!!

Everything went dark in the bays and I was alone there at the door. I opened my training manual to read, but, before long, the dreaded Lackland Lounge kicked off, and it soon got too loud—and too creepy—to read. The Lackland Lounge was what we called the ghost-like din of Airmen talking in their sleep. People under stress tend to talk a lot in their sleep, and that was proved almost every bloody night at Basic. It often got really, really noisy, and went on in an odd, graveyard symmetry where the seemingly choreographed cacophony of grunts, moans, shouts, chants, anguished cries, half-uttered mumbles, and other demonic noises made lights out a rather raucous and panic-filled situation.

And the Lounge wasn't all I had to endure. Outside, I could hear a commotion in the dorm across the hallway. My heart sunk. I knew a TI was in there lighting those unfortunate bastards up, and I knew it wouldn't be long before the TI finished with them and migrated across the hall to our dorm to have at us. I was in for a hard time. I got my pad of paper and pencil ready to take down whatever the TI commanded.

It was inevitable.

Sure enough, a few minutes later came a soul-shattering BOOM! BOOM! BOOM! from our door. The TI was there, ready to mess with us hard. I could see the shadow of his head through the blinds.

I pulled the blind aside—it was Staff Sergeant Eagan, our junior TI. Sergeant Eagan was a decent guy from Mississippi, but he could raise his fair share of Hell when he wanted to, and right now he wanted to.

He didn't look happy.

I followed procedures. I put my finger on the window over his nose, then I put my other finger over his name on the Authorized Personnel sheet. I then opened the door and Sergeant Eagan thundered in.

He made a beeline into the bays. Seconds later I heard the usual CLUNK! of beds being lifted and dropped hard to the floor—the dreaded 'Lackland Wake Up Call'. Eagan was rousting guys out of their racks at a furious pace.

And then…

"DORM GUARD!"

Oh crap, I was in for it now. "Proceeding!" I replied. I grabbed my pad and paper and scurried into the bay.

Sergeant Eagan was standing there, his flashlight beam poised at the wall.

"What the fuck is that, Dorm Guard?"

Centered in his flashlight was the electric razor, still plugged into the wall, still blinking merrily. It had taken him all of three minutes to find it.

"Sir, Airman Garcia reports as ordered! Sir, it's an electric razor, sir!" I replied.

"I can see that, godammit!" He then proceeded to berate me about the dangers of electrical devices left plugged into wall outlets. "There could be a fuckin' fire. Everybody could die, you stupid, trainee sumbitch!"

I foolishly then replied that the razor was fully UL rated, lab-tested, customer approved, and would not create a fire situation due to its design. Sergeant Eagan wasn't impressed. He then proceeded to uncover this whole 'razor conspiracy' and punish all players involved—me included. He soon discovered that the offending razor was owned by Airman DePierre, a wise apple from North Carolina, a guy who liked to crack jokes and pranks but always got caught and dogged up for them. Sergeant Eagan had DePierre up against the wall like a felon.

Sergeant Eagan then wanted to know who the previous Dorm Guard was so he could light him up too.

It was Airman Mallory, a little guy from New Mexico who, for whatever reason, the TI's couldn't stand. I knew when Mallory got involved, I was saved.

Mallory popped out of his bunk without wearing shoes, which was against regulations—you always had to have something on your feet when walking around. Sergeant Eagan was enraged and tried to stomp on his feet. Mallory had to dive out the way and take refuge in his rack to avoid getting stomped on.

Sergeant Eagan turned to me, shining his flashlight in my face. "Get your ass back to your station. I'll deal with you later, you dumb fuck!"

Thankfully, I did an about face and returned to my Dorm Guard cubbyhole.

Standing there by the door, I listened to Sergeant Eagan holding court in the bays, yelling at the top of his lungs, picking up bunks and dropping them, the beam of his flashlight waving around in the dark like a Sith light saber cutting off Jedi heads.

Two guys appeared in the corridor. It was DePierre and Mallory, followed by Sergeant Eagan. He placed the offending electric razor down in the center of the corridor. "Now, I want you two dumb asses to guard this fucking razor at the position of attention all fucking night long. This is Mission A #1 critical, got it?"

"Sir yes sir!" they replied.

"Fuckin' A! You better give thanks your fellow trainees aren't a pack of thieves! Do you two sumbitches understand me?

"Sir yes sir!"

He pointed at me. "See that trainee over there? He might not be too bright, and he might not give a Fuck! about your personal safety, but at least he's no thief."

"Sir yes sir!"

There was a pensive silence, then, Sergeant Eagan turned to deal with me.

He marched up.

"Ok, Mr. Not-So-Smart-Airman. I want you to write 100 times: '*I swear I will not allow my incompetence as an Airman to endanger the lives of my fellow trainees ever again.*' You will have these sentences accomplished by sun up, or your insufficient ass is going backwards, do you understand me, sir?"

"Sir yes sir!"

With that, he turned and went back into the bays to raise more Hell. I got out a fresh sheet of paper and started writing. Out of the corner of my eye, I could see DePierre and Mallory standing in their underwear at the position of attention with the razor on the floor between them like a giant, contoured dog turd.

A couple of guys, dragging blankets and pillows, emerged from the bay and marched into the latrine; from my position I couldn't tell who they were. Sergeant Eagan followed them. "You two Porky Pigs with the shitty footlockers and skid-marked drawers can get your shut-eye in the fuckin' shitter from now on, do you two understand me? Get your disgusting asses in there!"

They vanished into the latrine. Then Eagan turned to DePierre and Mallory. "Razor still there, you piss-poor Airmen?"

"Sir yes sir!"

"Razor not going anywhere, is it, you two IQ-Negative trainees?"

"Sir no sir!"

"Outstanding!"

He then handed the both of them a disposable razor and made them start dry shaving. "Here. Shave. Keep shaving. Don't stop!" DePierre and Mallory started shaving, I could see them both moving their hands about their faces in back and forth motions as if they were fanning themselves.

Then, he came at me again. I just stood there writing my sentences. He got so close, his nose was pressed up against my ear, snorting searing hot dragon breath into the side of my face with serial killer rapidity. I roasted in his hot nose breath.

I knew the best thing to do in a situation like this would be to maintain my military bearing and ignore the Sergeant. I just kept on writing, staring at my paper, saying nothing. If he audibly addressed me, then I would respond with the proper military greeting, but, until he did that, I would continue ignoring him.

It worked!! He eventually went away, leaving me to write sentences like a school boy wearing a DUNCE hat.

"Keep shaving, you fucks!" he yelled at DePierre and Mallory. He opened the door to the latrine. "You two Porky Pigs all tucked in?"

"Sir yes sir!" I heard in tandem from the latrine.

"Good! Nighty night!"

Soon, he allowed DePierre and Mallory to return to their bunks. He departed, and I finished my eventful Dorm Guard shift without further incident.

In the morning, as I dressed, I heard Sergeant Eagan cry out "GARCIA!" Sighing, I went to the office to find out what he wanted. There he was, morning fresh, holding a steaming cup of coffee.

"Airman, the penmanship in your sentences is completely unacceptable bullshit, do you understand me, sir? You will re-accomplish these sentences, only you will turn in 200 legible sentences instead of 100, right?"

"Sir yes sir!"

"Dismissed."

So, I redid my sentences, turned them back in, only this time with better penmanship. The incident was forgotten and I made it the rest of the way pretty much without a hitch. I still remember DePierre and Mallory standing there in their shorts, guarding the electric razor and dry-shaving their foolish faces, making swishing motions with their hands as they shaved.

Just goes to show you: *Everything's a big deal at Basic Training*

ADDITIONAL PHOTO GALLERY

View from behind the Base HQ looking east across a small park towards Commerce Drive. An abstract, somewhat prehistoric-looking sculpture featuring an eagle's nest and inscription sits in the center of the park. In the far distance, on the other side of Pacesetter Drive, is Hangar 2. White Hall once blocked the view of Hangar 2 from this spot, but has since been torn down in 2016, leaving a large green empty hole. (RDG)

Above: A gothic wasteland, the Base Hospital in 2012, a FOR SALE sign in red letters nailed to a tree

Below: The rear of the hospital, like a turn of the century consumption sanitarium (RDG)

Above: An incredible weed field obscures Faktor Hall, home of Matt Fujimoto and the 72nd Squadron.

Below: A similar situation in the courtyard of the 42nd Squadron. The dayroom can be seen behind the pile of brush. (RDG)

Above: Chanute's venerable 40's era water tower looming over the old Fire House. The water tower is one of
the few things still in-use at the base.

Below: After a rainstorm, the eerie desolation behind
White Hall near the Hangars. (RDG)

Above: The massive corpse of White Hall, displaying the sheer size and sprawl of the building, a ghost-hunter's paradise.

Below: Behind White Hall near the old gymnasium. There were piles of tires stacked up in and around the building everywhere. (RDG)

Above: The spectacularly unsafe main door to White Hall, the overhang audibly groaning after a rainstorm in 2012.

Below: White Hall, just in a sad state all the way around. (RDG)

A crazy-weird sculpture in a park situated behind the Base HQ. On the other side is an inscription reading: *"We will have turned the corner when we have reached the point where others turn and regard us as pacesetters."*

Base HQ's main door. Over the door is the seal of Chanute Technical Training Center. It features three plumes and the Lamp of Knowledge. Above is a fist holding a key. The phrase "*Sustineo Alas*" means "Sustain the Wings" or, more simply "Keep `em Flying".

Above: The Borman Gate with its missile. When the base was in operation, there was a fence with a guard shack situated by the road.

Below: Grissom Hall, one of the hangars near the tarmac. (RDG)

Main door of the Base Hospital (RDG)

Shop on the corner of Eagle and Flessner where the Author took most of his Jetmech classes. Though it isn't in the frame, most of the metal siding of the building is blowing loose in the wind. (RDG)

**COMING SOON
FROM REN GARCIA**

LEAGUE of ELDER

THE HOUSE of BLOODSTEIN

mentralysis

REN GARCIA

What should have been obvious to Lord Kabyl from
the start at last becomes crystal clear: Foolish is he
who dares possess the Ultimate Object, for misery
shall be his only reward.

LEAGUE OF ELDER

6TH TURN: KAT

REN GARCIA

Lord Belmont's life ended in Clovis, in the impenetrable darkness beneath the ground where forbidden rites were once held. Lady Gwendolyn was his love, body and soul, and the Demon in Blue Light killed her.

Every year, on the anniversary of Gwen's death, he returns to Clovis to stand in the cold desolation, hearing the wind moan through the lonely passes, feeling her loss all over again.

On this anniversary, he wasn't alone in Clovis. He hears the noises rustling in the brush. He smells the raw river of Shadow tech. Then he sees it:

The claws …

The flicking tail …

The maniacal, glittering eyes fixed on him …

"I've been waiting for you," it says in a grating voice as it attacks.

* * * * *

Far away, across the cosmos in a city of wondrous crystal towers, two people watch in horror as the desperate scene at Clovis unfolds. They had worked so hard, sacrificed so much, even argued for it before the gods. They convinced the gods they were right, that they knew best, and everything would go well.

But, things weren't going well at Clovis.

If this situation turns out poorly, then ages worth of work would be lost, and, just possibly, the universe itself might come to an end.

ABOUT THE AUTHOR

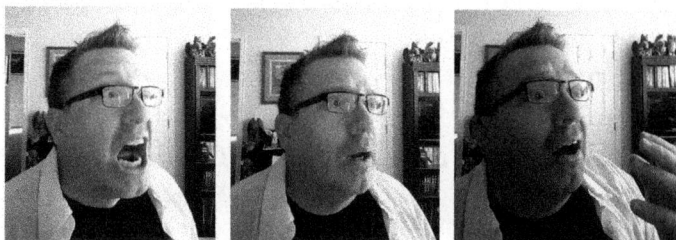

Ren Garcia, the author of the League of Elder Series, graduated from the Ohio State University with a degree in literature. He enjoys playing volleyball, urban exploration, taking pictures of clouds, and ice hockey. He lives in Columbus, Ohio, with his wife and their four vivacious little wiener dogs. You can visit Ren's website/on-line glossary at:

http://www.thetempleoftheexplodinghead.com

Bibliography

Anderson, Nancy. "Chanute Grows Rapidly as War Approaches." *The Rantoul Press and Chanute Field News: Commemorative Edition,* June 14, 1976.

Hansen G, Fred. "Ordeal to Last a Decade." *The Rantoul Press and Chanute Field News: Commemorative Edition,* June 14, 1976.

Hanson D, Mark, *Images of America: Rantoul and Chanute Air Force Base.* 72, 98-107 Charlston: Arcadia 2011.

Podagrosi B, Katy,. *Eye of the Storm, Chanute Closes.* Paxton, Illinois, Paxton Printing company, 2000.

Manning, Thomas A. (2005), History of Air Education and Training Command, 1942–2002. Office of History and Research, Headquarters, AETC, Randolph AFB, Texas ASIN: B000NYX3PC

www.ingramcontent.com/pod-product-compliance
Lightning Source LLC
Chambersburg PA
CBHW061750020426
42331CB00006B/1419